Faith, Hope and Charity as Character Traits in Adler's Individual Psychology

With Related Essays in Spirituality and Phenomenology

Allan Maurice Savage
Sheldon William Nicholl

with a contribution by
Erik Mansager

University Press of America,® Inc.
Lanham · Boulder · New York · Toronto · Oxford

Copyright © 2003 by
University Press of America,® Inc.
4501 Forbes Boulevard
Suite 200
Lanham, Maryland 20706
UPA Acquisitions Department (301) 459-3366

PO Box 317
Oxford
OX2 9RU, UK

ISBN 0-7618-2639-4 (paperback : alk. ppr.)

CONTENTS

PART TWO

RELATED ESSAYS IN PHENOMENOLOGY AND SPIRITUALITY

Contents

FOREWORD

This academic exploration presents a new way of thinking. It is accomplished not by abandoning the past, but rather by understanding its underlying mysteries to help guide us into a positive future. So much has been said about the global village in terms of finance and economy, yet people are often blind to the fact that it will be harmonious social relationships that will grant the world a future worthy of the human intellect. Mankind must learn to achieve balance in our existence as individuals. The strength of a global community is determined by the spiritual health of its members and moulded upon an emerging understanding of the integration of theology, science and philosophy. This book reflects exactly this type of integration with ideas and notions beyond present understanding. The author, A. M. Savage, is a published academic theologian who approaches intellectual and scholarly pursuits from an unusual perspective. His accessibility of thought and energetic discourse will be attractive to readers in a wise range of disciplines. This is evidenced by the co-authorship of S. Nicholl and the contribution of E. Mansager. These are scholars of different professions, academic credentials and ages, drawn together by their shared interest in this unique exploration.

I have read the essays in this volume. Although many of them stand independently, I suggest that the reader partake of them in their entirety. The thoughts that arise in the individual essays are expanded and developed in others. These ideas are sure to inspire. The discussion about poets and mystics as phenomenological thinkers has kindled my interest into the mind of the poet – an area which I originally had believed to be very distant from this discussion . The remarkable research of the authors is obvious and provides a wealth of resources.

The organization of the book into parts is purposeful and constructive. The first part begins with a description of Adler's life and his psychological theories. It continues with chapters highlighting the positive nature of Adlerian psychology and its compatibility with contemporary pastoral theology. The last chapter in this portion of the book is an engaging explication of the virtues: faith, hope and charity. The authors present this information in a style which is comfortable for both the general and informed reader.

The beginning chapters ease the reader into the more challenging features of the second part of the book where the examination of Adlerian thinking involves a unique application of principles. This portion has substantive ideas and requires more than a cursory read. The continued dialogue between Savage and various authors is comparable to participation in a discussion forum in which mutual respect and openness define the experience.

There has been a loss of faith in the future. The present contains for many an immensely skewed perception of what is truly important to the spiritual well-being of the individual and the communities to which they belong. We are living in an age when faith, hope and charity are viewed as quaint virtues from the past and ill-suited to contemporary application. This book clearly illustrates that this is not the case. Written with unerring intellect, it offers a new threshold of thinking to which the reader has been invited to listen, ponder and institute.

Anita Oja

PREFACE

This undertaking is co-authored by a theologian and psychologist as an interdisciplinary consideration of the virtues of faith, hope and charity. That theologians and psychologists have collaborated with each other in addressing the spiritual well-being of the individual in community is nothing new. This continues through traditional ways of thinking. However, in the years following WWII collaborative thinking as a contemporary way forward has become more popular. Currently, there is renewed interest in the individual as person as the common subject of theology and psychology.

Pastoral theology has been influenced by cognitive therapy and this work is a deliberate attempt to understand the virtues of faith, hope and charity through cognitive therapy. Cognitive therapy as a conscious knowledgeable intervention is intended to empower persons for action and to enable virtuous action by individuals. Three virtues are considered from the perspective of Alfred Adler's Individual Psychology since it is a form of cognitive therapy. Faith, as an act of commitment, arises out of the innate striving for the need of community feeling. Hope acts in the present moment and strives to improve upon community feeling. Charity, or charitable co-operation with the other brings about a healthy lifestyle. An investigative appreciation of the influence of Alfred Adler's cognitive therapy on the theological virtues is the thrust of Part One of this work.

ACKNOWLEDGMENTS

No writing is undertaken in a vacuum. Many individuals, in various and sundry ways, have influenced the notions and ideas discussed in this book. As principal author, I acknowledge my indebtedness to these individuals, many of whom I no longer see. Sheldon Nicholl, the co-author, was an inspiration for me in that, being able to share in a creative venture with a "young mind," I found this book a joy to produce. The discussions with students enrolled in the Faculty of Theology (University of Winnipeg), whom I taught in Thunder Bay, helped me refine and clarify some of my ideas. Leo Oja, has served as a faithful "sounding board" over the years for the ideas that eventually took shape in this work – including those in Part Two of this work. I am grateful that Erik Mansager agreed to reproduce our "collaborative exchange" originally appearing in the Year Book 2000 of the Adlerian Society of the United Kingdom. Michele Verdenik, through her word processing and computer skills, lightened the task of preparing the text for publication and Mentor Computers, Thunder Bay, Ontario provided, *pro bono*, valuable technical advice. Finally, I am grateful to William Frost, PhD, editor of *Explorations: Journal for Adventurous Thought*, whose choice to publish some of my original essays gave me the confidence to continue in an academic writing career. Notwithstanding many other contributions to and influences on my thinking I am solely responsible, unless otherwise stated, for the ideas as they appear here in print.

CHAPTER 1

ALFRED ADLER: HIS LIFE, A MODEL OF THE THEORY

Alfred Adler was a brilliant psychiatrist who had amazing insights into the nature of personality development. Despite facing many adverse conditions as a child and growing up amidst political and social strife, Adler used these negative energies and refocussed them into many more positive ideas and influences. How did one man become so great? Could it be that he came from good genetic stock that naturally predisposed him toward intellectual greatness? Perhaps his environment was one so positive that it would make the behaviorist John B. Watson blush? We briefly sketch Adler's life from childhood to adulthood, ailing and insecure child to loving husband, frustrated schoolboy to successful doctor and theorist.

Adler's own life is a ready-made example of theory put into practice. When formulating his theory of personality, he drew extensively from his own life experiences. The following is a depiction of Adler's life "in a nutshell." Many of the concepts mentioned in the next chapter fit aspects of Adler's life perfectly and both chapters taken as a whole help tie all these concepts together. Some readers might find it useful to re-read this chapter once they have become familiar with Adler's personality theory and its concepts.

Alfred Adler was born the second of six children in Rudolfsheim, Austria on February 7, 1870. As a child he was communicative and easily made friends, rarely seeking solitude. However, Adler often had solitude thrust upon him in one way or another throughout his childhood. Looking at his childhood, one sees a life marked by illness. He would suffer a

spasm of the glottis when he became angry, which often created a severe shortness of breath. This cond
ition was so harrowing that, at age three, Adler decided to not get angry anymore, relieving himself of the agonizing condition.

Adler suffered from rickets so he could not play games with other children. Because of his condition, Adler received a lot of special treatment, but this stopped when his younger brother was born. He was jealous of his older brother (ironically named Sigmund). Adler could not do the things his brother did because he was so frail; this made him feel inferior to his older brother. Being the first-born male offspring, Sigmund held a position generally considered to be of high status in Jewish households. Sigmund was bright and domineering; so much so that Alfred usually felt like he was engaged in a fight for their parents' attention.

Adler's childhood was also marked by death. At age four, he watched his younger brother, Rudolf, die of diphtheria in bed next to him, an event that was quite traumatic for him. A year later, Adler went skating with an older boy. During this time they became separated and Adler was left on his own. He was lost and became very cold. Somehow he found his way home, developed pneumonia, and nearly died. In fact, the first doctor to attend to him gave his condolences to Adler's parents for he expected Alfred would not survive. Sometime after his bout of pneumonia, Adler decided he would become a doctor. As Grey (1998,1) put it, this decision was "a vindication of one of his earliest concepts — intellectual compensation over physical inferiorities."

As a youngster, Adler enjoyed school and did well until he had to start in Gymnasium, which roughly corresponded to the fourth grade in modern North American comparison. Adler soon felt inferior at school because he had only mediocre grades. He was particularly bad at mathematics, a course that he failed in his first year in Gymnasium. At one point his father threatened to remove him from school and apprentice him to a cobbler, since academics seemed to be an unrealistic pursuit. The threat apparently worked; he worked hard and brought up all of his grades. One day he successfully solved a particularly difficult problem to which no one, his teacher included, seemed to be able to find a solution. This event inspired Adler with confidence; where once there was fear and trepidation, there now only remained a new-found interest in mathematics and he resolved to improve his skills. Adler eventually became first in his class for mathematics! Later in life Adler noted that the experience helped him "to see the fallacy of theories of special talents or inborn capacities" (Hoffman 1994,15).

In 1888, Adler enrolled in medical school at the University of Vienna.

Once again Adler's detestation for formal schools shone through. He did only the bare minimum number of courses possible to get through medical school, obligatory courses necessary to pass the three qualifying exams that would grant him his degree. Adler passed all three exams with the grade of "adequate," which was the lowest possible passing grade. He received his medical degree on November 22, 1895.

During his young adulthood, Adler became involved in politics. His socialist orientation began with an interest in Marx and Engels. As Hoffman (1994, 22) noted, these writers "seemed to offer a real path for actualizing his idealistic ambition to help humanity through medical intervention". The socialist movement in Vienna allowed him an outlet to strive for goals like economic justice and concern for the disadvantaged. Also, it served as a way of opposing the German Nationalist movement that harbored an anti-Semitic stance, which was not unique to that political party at the time.

In the summer of 1897, Adler met and fell in love with Russian Jewish-born Raissa Timofeivna Epstein. They were married in Smolensk, Russia on December 23, 1897. Seven and a half months later, on August 5, 1898, their first child, Valentine Dina Adler, was born. No one is quite sure if Valentine was a premature baby or if Raissa was pregnant before the wedding. After the birth of their second child, Alexandra, on September 24, 1901 Raissa began to feel overburdened and marital strain became evident. Raissa was fiercely independent, intellectual, and politically active. She was a passionate feminist who disliked domesticity. Rather, she preferred the company of like-minded women who were themselves intelligent and politically active socialists. Raissa was the "complete antithesis of the subservient housewife" (Hoffman 1994, 48). The Adlers managed to make their marriage work despite the fact that both would go on to have very busy careers and political interests. Their third child, Kurt, was born February 25, 1905. Cornelia, their forth and final child, was born on October 18, 1909. Throughout the entire time they were married, and despite spending many months apart in the latter part of Adler's career and the obvious tension their political and professional lives created between them, there was no indication of infidelity on behalf of either Alfred or Raissa.

Adler saw his first psychiatric patient as an independent practitioner shortly after his wedding. The lady was Adler's distant cousin who came to him complaining of a headache. Adler pointed out that people do not develop headaches independent of contextual forces and gently inquired as to whether she was happily married. The woman resented the implication and stormed out of the office. However, she applied for a divorce about a month later. Adler saw a group of clients employed as entertainers (e.g., strongmen, trapeze artists, acrobats) with Prater's Amusement Park. It was during this time that Adler began to seriously consider the unaccountable link between mind and body. Reflecting on the backgrounds of his clients he found that many of the park's entertainers had at one time "suffered from a congenital weakness early in life and then strove successfully to overcome it through athletic prowess" (Hoffman 1994, 33). No doubt such reflections led Adler to conceive of the notions of organ inferiority, compensation, and overcompensation, concepts which we discuss in the next chapter.

In 1898, Adler wrote a thirty-one-page monograph, which dealt with the health conditions of tailors. In the book, *Health Book for the Tailor Trade*, he described first the deplorable conditions under which many tailors worked. The second section described many of the diseases and ailments (i.e., pulmonary tuberculosis, arthritis, rheumatism, scoliosis) which led to higher mortality rates in tailors. The final section argued for new health legislation and made suggestions as to what should be included in this proposal. The overall work became representative of Adler's work throughout his life: highly innovative theory presented in an easy-to-read, easy-to-understand, jargon-free, non-technical format. It also foreshadowed Adler's passion for social reformation.

The Freudian Years

In November of 1902, Adler received a postcard from the famous Viennese psychiatrist, Sigmund Freud, inviting Adler to join his small group of professional colleagues who met on a weekly basis. The postcard read (as cited in Hoffman 1994, 42):

> Very honoured Sir Colleague:
> A small circle of colleagues and followers is going to give me the pleasure of meeting at my house once a week in the evening at half past eight in order to discuss the themes which interest us, psychology and neuropathology. I know of Reitler, Max Kahan, and Stekel. Will you have the goodness to join? We have agreed upon next Thursday, and I am expecting your kind answer whether you would like to come and whether this evening would suit you. With hearty greetings as your colleague,
> DR. FREUD

Interestingly, this weekly group later became known as the Wednesday Psychological Society. Contrary to popular belief it was Freud who approached Adler and not the converse. This would be a point which

Adler would later make known with great vehemence on his American tours in the 1920s since many would refer to him as Freud's "pupil," a thorn which would stick in Adler's side throughout his scholarly career.

Another point of interest is that no one really knows how Adler and Freud actually met. That is, what inspired Freud to make this first contact? There are two popular speculations here. The first one suggests that Adler wrote an article defending Freud's book, *The Interpretation of Dreams*, from ridicule in a scholarly journal, *Neu Freie Pressse*. In gratitude, Freud wrote the postcard inviting Adler to join his circle. The only problem with this account is that no such article nor letter was written by Adler for this (or any other) journal. The second account of how Adler came to join Freud's circle came from Freud himself. Freud insisted that the original five members, of which Adler was the fifth and youngest, were admirers of his theories and sought him out. Likewise, loyal Freudians would describe Adler as a pupil or disciple of Freud and insist that Adler was overambitious and ungrateful for the guidance Freud had given him in his early years. This account is inaccurate and does not account for the postcard inviting Adler to join the group. The explanation posited today is that Freud most likely heard of Adler's growing reputation as a skilled and knowledgeable physician with many progressive ideas.

Although Adler was regarded as the most creative and articulate thinker of the Wednesday Psychological Society, he and Freud never became close socially. The foundation of their relationship was built on mutual respect and was, therefore, one of professional colleagues. On the surface, they had many apparent commonalities. Both grew up in Jewish households which had immigrated to Vienna. Neither had interest in observing Jewish customs and rituals and considered themselves secularists. In fact, Adler formally abandoned Judaism on October 17, 1904, which is hardly surprising given the anti-Semitic atmosphere prevalent in Austro-Hungary. Both men's fathers were nonintellectual merchants who provided unstable income for their families. Adler and Freud never socialized outside their weekly meetings despite this common background. Several factors probably kept the men from developing a relationship beyond their academic association. First, there was an age gap that was quite large, though not large enough for Freud to assume a true father figure role (which he would later claim he held). Second, Freud preferred an aristocratic social circle whereas Adler preferred the working-classes. Third, Freud was academically oriented; he preferred research and saw professional practice as a necessity only insofar as it paid his bills. Adler's primary focus was that of a clinical professional and he rather detested research. Professional practice was where his brilliance shone brightest, with his outgoing, friendly disposition and ability to gain insight into the true nature of his patients' conditions within a relatively short assessment period.

In November, 1906 Adler gave a major presentation entitled "On the Organic Bases of Neurosis" which would serve bas the basis for his upcoming book, *A Study of Organ Inferiority*. Several main points were outlined in this presentation. The concept of *organ inferiority* was introduced. Adler argued that the majority of neuroses derived from congenital weakness (as he found with his clients from the amusement park). The concept of *compensation* was also introduced. All persons strive to overcome their organ inferiority in a struggle for social adaptation. Adler also noted that sometimes individuals can exaggerate this need to triumph over inferiority in a processes he called *overcompensation*. Several months later, in 1907, *A Study of Organ Inferiority* was published. The book's implicit point: "If compensation and overcompensation are such basic human characteristics, then there must exist a natural, inborn drive for mastery and competence" (Hoffman 1994, 57). Adler developed his theory further with the notion of *masculine protest*, which would become one of the basic tenets of his 1912 book, *The Neurotic Constitution*, which would focus on the early sense of inferiority that developed soon after birth. From then on, the difference between Freud's and Adler's views became steadily more marked. Adler had never fully accepted Freud's original theories that mental difficulties were caused exclusively by a sexual trauma and he opposed the generalizations when dreams were interpreted, in each instance, as sexual wish fulfilment. "The essential battle between Freud and Adler . . . was not over power or personality, but intensely different ideas" (Hoffman 1994, 69). After prolonged discussions, each of the two men tried to win the other over to his own point of view, a futile effort at best, which culminated when Freud implemented a carefully constructed plan to oust Adler from the Wednesday Psychological Society. Adler left Freud's circle in 1911 with a group of eight colleagues and formed his own group called the Society for Free Psychoanalytic Study, later to become the Society for Individual Psychology in 1913.

Moving Beyond Psychoanalysis and Toward Individual Psychology

The year 1912 saw the publication of Adler's next major work, *The Neurotic Constitution*. Several of the ideas presented in this book agreed with the basic tenets of Freud's theories. For example, Adler argued that personality is shaped in early childhood and relatively difficult to change after age five. However, rather than focussing on psychosexual stages as Freud did, Adler focussed on psychosocial development. Like Freud, Adler argued that the "inner world" of the mind is largely hidden from consciousness. However, Adler argued that, rather than requiring extensive sessions of *free association* (the technique used by Freud), one's everyday behaviours reveal hidden feelings, beliefs, and desires. Similar to Freud, Adler also noted that trained professionals can help individuals gain insight into the hidden world of the mind. The overall driving force behind personality development was not sexual in nature, rather it derived from a sense of inferiority, a sense of inadequacy relative to one's environmental context. As previously mentioned, the topics of compensation, overcompensation, and masculine protest were explored as well as *fictional finalism*, Adler's term referring to the fact that many of the goals in life or solutions to feeling inferior were largely fictional rather than objective realities. The ways in which one strove for mastery in the world (later to be called *lifestyles*) substantiated one's personality.

Adler was drafted into service in 1916 during World War I where he served as a military physician. During this time, Adler was horrified by the tactics the military used to get wounded soldiers back onto the battlefield. For example, army psychiatrists (not including Adler) would try to convince soldiers that it would be easier for them to go back to the trenches than suffer the anxiety of post-battlefield trauma. To this end, the soldiers would be forced to undergo a variety of "treatments" like repeated cold showers, mock surgeries, and being locked in isolation chambers. All these "treatments" were designed to get the men back into action to fight, what was then, a losing battle. Late into his tour, Adler no longer saw service as a patriotic duty. This traumatic experience spurred his interest concerning the psychological causes of war. Perhaps more importantly, it was during and immediately following this time that Adler's theory of *social feeling* began to take shape. According to Hoffman (1994, 101), to Adler, "it now seemed indisputable that what civilization needed was not more individualism but more *social feeling*: compassion, altruism, and selflessness." He would refine his concept of social feeling through numerous discussions in Viennese coffeehouses with friends and with professional colleagues, eventually making it perhaps the most fundamental and paramount concept of his Individual Psychology.

Around 1919 and the early 1920s Adler really began to become known for his contributions to child and family psychology. He even went so far as to make himself available, free of charge, to teachers seeking advice about how to handle difficult students. Adler also conducted sessions whereby selected children and their families underwent therapy in front of a group of other families and teachers. Amazingly, not only did the teachers and families learn more about personality theory, they received effective psychotherapy. This system of "school-guidance clinics" was not without its criticisms. The majority of psychologists cited three concerns: 1) The public nature of the sessions was seen as inappropriate and perhaps even harmful to the children. 2) Adler did not keep rigorous statistics — a personal prejudice, which would plague Adler throughout his career. 3) There were no follow-up sessions to evaluate the long-standing effectiveness (if any) of the interventions. Despite these criticisms, Adler would influence social policy in Vienna and the surrounding area, advocating psychoeducation for teachers and parents and more services for troubled youth.

Adler had several successful lecture tours of the U.S. The first tour began in the fall of 1926 and ended in the spring of 1927; the second tour began in February, 1928 and ended in the fall of 1928; his third tour went from January, 1929 to the summer of that same year. Around the time of these tours, the U.S. was undergoing a shift in social climate. Organized religion was suffering due to the focus on science, which parallelled a revolution in social values pertaining to romance, marriage, and sexual behaviour. Adler's ideas regarding these three values were acceptable to the American public since Adler appeared to be rooted in medical science. His ideas were not so radical that they were deemed unpalatable by those with conservative views. Rather, he presented a conventional view of marriage that was somewhat paradoxically conservative and progressive. He suggested that monogamy was not obsolete nor could it be replaced by a new style of adult relationship. Hoffman (1994, 213) noted that Adler once stated that

> love is the basis of all our culture . . . and without it, our present civilization would collapse. Monogamy is the highest form of love. I have no patience with the movements to make love easier. If it is made too easy, it degenerates into cheap pleasure.

However, definitely obsolete and irrelevant was the traditional male attitude of the "double standard" whereby extramarital sex was acceptable for the husband only and the wife was a husband's servant or property. This difference also reflected Adler's and Freud's personal lives and their differing attitudes toward the U.S. in general and its cultural norms. Adler was very pro-American, seeing as a land of opportunity and where a fledgling society (compared to that of Europe) could avoid the errors of the past in the "Old World" by focussing on the health and education of children, and the family in general, from the outset. He began to move away from his socialist ideals spurred by the corruption of communism and the apparent intellectual, occupational, and personal freedom offered by America's capitalism. Adler was not without his reservations, however. He thought that Americans were so caught up in occupational and personal success that child rearing seemed to suffer, which would lead to longstanding difficulties not unlike those Adler had observed a few decades ago before in Austria. Unlike Adler, Freud was very anti-American. He held traditional views and felt uneasy about the elevated standing American women held relative to European women. He also resented the fact that Adler had won financial backing from American philanthropist, Charles Henry Davis. Adding insult to injury, Freud's book, *The Interpretation of Dreams*, would only sell about twenty thousand copies whereas Adler's book sales for *Understanding Human Nature* would number in the hundreds of thousands.

Interestingly, the latter years of Adler's publishing career were, paradoxically, marked by a drastic reduction in time dedicated to writing. Rather, he contracted out to freelance writers who used his lecture notes as templates from which they would construct new texts. The vast majority of these lectures were given after he moved to the U.S. in the fall of 1929. Starting with *Understanding Human Nature*, Adler's involvement in this process diminished from publication to publication. Adler was never very interested in writing and did not consider himself to be primarily an academic. He was a clinician and it was in his practice that he could implement his theories and collect new "data" (although he seldom ever used statistical data in his articles and books). However, he published prolifically during the years in which he lived in the U.S. (e.g., 1930 saw the publication of several books and articles). As well, Adler enjoyed professorships at a number of institutions like the New School for Social Research (where he taught his first course in the U.S. in 1928), Columbia University (1929-1930), and Long Island College of Medicine (1931-1937).

In the preface to *Understanding Human Nature*, Adler (1927, 245) claimed that the "purpose of the book is to point how the mistaken behaviour of the individual affects the harmony of our social community." He noted how personality was fixed at an early age and difficulties in adult life arose from faulty problem solving strategies developed in childhood, but these could be modified with help from a psychotherapist (concepts to be discussed in chapter 2). Perhaps his most profound, and yet non-acclaimed, idea was that it "is not our *objective* experiences which bring us from the straight path of development, but our personal *attitude* and *evaluation* of events, and the *manner* in which we evaluate and weigh occurrences." This idea is now accepted with little controversy in modern psychology and is generally attributed to cognitive therapist Albert Ellis, pioneer of Rational Emotive Therapy.

The Pattern of Life, (1930) essentially presented twelve case studies. Each case described or dealt with a different problem to be examined and treated. These were childhood cases where it became apparent that the father-child bond was particularly weak, a concept not considered to be of particular importance to Freud and psychoanalysts of the time (Hoffman 1995, 237). Published later that same year, *The Science of Living* had great appeal to American readers. Hoffman noted that it gave "the widespread impression that science (rather than religion) could now provide people with true insights for happiness and self-fulfilment" It was the text in which Adler coined the term *life-style* for the first time, although he had used similar terms (e.g., life-plan, guiding image) in previous books.

In 1931, *What Life Should Mean to You* was published. It submitted insights on academic, vocational, and family issues that commonly affected adults. Two concepts were presented that were significant at that time. The first was his continued support of the institution of marriage. Adler (1931, 276) claimed:

> In our present day civilization, people are often not well prepared for cooperation. Our training has been too much towards individual[ism]. . . . [Most adults] are unaccustomed to consulting another human being's interests and aims, desires, hopes and ambitions. They are not prepared for the problems of a common task.

Social interest and marriage went hand-in-hand since one needed strong social interest to mature personally and adjust socially. Likewise, a successful marriage depended on genuine concern for one's partner and offspring in the true altruistic sense and not viewing them as a means to satisfy one's own needs and desires. Second, Adler basically rejected the idea that personality was totally heritable. During a time when the eugenics movement was becoming popular (and powerful, especially with respect to the concept of intelligence), Adler had the courage and foresight to note systemic influences that were perhaps more powerful than any heritable characteristics. As long as children were brought up with sufficient self esteem, *social tolerance*, co-operativeness, and encouragement, their possibilities for the future were infinite.

In 1934 Adler made sure that the rest of his family left Vienna. Always an astute observer of political events and influences, he noticed the fascist Nazi regime's rocketing (and violent) rise to power. He foresaw another war, a war that could resemble the Great War he fought in, which was something no one, especially his family, should have to witness or live through. As well, he saw America as *the* place to live and work and he longed for his family to join him. He enjoyed teaching and lecturing, and his children, Alexandra and Kurt, even attended these lectures from time to time. In fact, in 1937 he planned to deliver a series of lectures in England with his daughter, Alexandra, at the universities of London and Exeter. However, this was never to come to pass. On May 28, 1937, on the last day of a series of lectures at Aberdeen University before he was to travel to London, he went for a walk after breakfast. He collapsed shortly thereafter and was found unconscious, but still breathing, on the street. Alfred Adler died of a heart attack. He was sixty-seven years old.

Alfred Adler's life became a model for his theory of personality. His physiological maladies are a perfect illustration of his concept of organ inferiority. His theory on the effects of birth order can clearly be seen in his childhood relationship with his older brother. Both of these became sources for Adler's feelings of inferiority which motivated him throughout his lifetime. As well, he knew first-hand what it was like to be dethroned from a position of privilege within the family. From an early age Adler was afraid and intimidated by death. His striving for superiority in eventually becoming a doctor not only demonstrated his concept of social interest, but also his concept of fictional finalism. Becoming a doctor specializing in incurable diseases was his way of becoming a socially useful type of person with a lot of social tolerance. His involvement in the Great War convinced him that highly developed social interest, a basic tenet of Individual Psychology, offered the best hope for establishing a world based on co-operation rather than competition. This "snap-shot" of Alfred Adler's life is but the "tip of the iceberg" in beginning to understand how his life influenced his theory. At first glance this might appear to be an example of what social psychologists call the *false consensus effect* whereby one overestimates the commonality of one's opinions and experiences. However, many of Adler's premises have held up over the years. What is perhaps most interesting is not that Adler developed a theory based on his own experiences that he thought would apply to people in general, but that he was, in many respects, correct!

CHAPTER 2

THE INDIVIDUAL PSYCHOLOGY OF ALFRED ADLER

Ego Psychology

Alfred Adler belonged to a class of personality theorists called *ego psychologists*. This term derives from the fact that these theorists believed that the ego existed at birth separate from the *id* (rather than developing from the *id*) and had its own source of energy. Freud believed that the major function of the ego was to mediate between the *id* and the superego and external reality. Ego psychologists believed that the ego did much more than that. According to ego psychology, the ego's most important role was to help the individual fit better into the world through the process of adaptation. The desires of the *id* were no longer seen as the sole cause of motivation. There could be other sources of motivation and, according to some theorists, the development and maturation process the ego undergoes as the person develops was of primary concern and determined personality in and of itself. Adler is one of the most well-known of all the former colleagues of Sigmund Freud. Often called neo-Freudians, theorists like Adler, Jung, and Horney studied with Freud for a time and then broke away from Freud (usually because they felt he overemphasized sexuality) to develop their own theories. In order to understand better Adler's personality theory, a review of Freud's general theory of the mind is necessary.

Freud envisioned a "topography" of the mind consisting of three parts: conscious, preconscious, and unconscious. An iceberg is commonly used as a visual aid, helping one track the relative size and importance of these parts. Freud thought of the *conscious* much the same as a layperson would. It was the part of the mind that contains the information of which one is currently aware. "People typically can verbalize about their conscious experience and can think about it in a logical way" (Carver & Scheier 1996, 201). Using the iceberg analogy, the conscious would be the part of the iceberg floating above the water. Just below the conscious was the *preconscious*, which was basically one's memory. It contained the thoughts, beliefs, and ideas that were not presently in conscious thought, but could be brought into awareness with a little effort. For example, most everyone knows his or her phone number, but it is not always part of conscious thought. Bringing this information from memory to awareness is an example of bringing information from the preconscious to the conscious. Continuing with the iceberg analogy, the preconscious would comprise the area of the iceberg submerged just beneath the surface of the water. It can be seen through the water and one is aware that it is there. The final aspect of Freud's topography of the mind was the *unconscious*. It was not directly accessible by conscious thought. The unconscious was considered a storehouse for urges, feelings, and ideas that are associated with anxiety, conflict, or pain. These forces exert an enduring influence on later actions and conscious experiences. Completing the iceberg analogy, the unconscious would be represented by the part of the iceberg completely submerged beneath the water and which is no longer visible from the surface. It composes about 80%-90% of the iceberg's mass, but people are largely unaware of its presence and importance in its overall composition.

Similar to his topography of the mind, Freud conceived of three components of personality. The *id* was thought to be present from birth and was the root of all the basic desires and motivation (e.g., hunger, sleep, sex). It operated on the pleasure principle; all needs are to be instantly gratified without regard to external circumstances. The *ego* was the second psychological function and developed from the *id*. It operated on the reality principle. That is, its purpose was to satisfy the needs and desires of the *id* effectively, but also take into account external constraints on behaviour. The *superego* was Freud's term for the third component of personality. The superego encompassed societal values impressed upon an individual by the parents (i.e., rules for good behaviour, standards of excellence, sense of justice). In everyday language, the superego is one's conscience. Both the ego and superego developed and derived their energy from the *id.*

Origins of the Inferiority Complex

According to Adler, to be human means to feel inferior. Therefore, *feelings of inferiority* are always present. Because these feelings are common to everyone, they should not be seen as weakness. These feelings are the forces that determine our behaviour. These inferiorities may be imagined or real. These feelings begin in infancy because early in life individuals are totally helpless. In comparison to children, adults have power and are strong. Even as infants, individuals are aware of this and realize there is no point in trying to overcome it. As a result, children learn to accept this inferiority. This is not genetically based; it applies to everyone because it is a function of a common environment. Adler claimed that these feelings were necessary to grow, develop, and mature. Maturation occurs as individuals try to get past these feelings of inferiority.

Feelings of inferiority continue to intensify throughout life. When these feelings become so strong that they are overwhelming, difficulties arise. Adler envisioned these difficulties as constituting a syndrome that he called an *inferiority complex*, an inability to solve life's problems. People suffering from an inferiority complex feel helpless, have poor opinions of themselves, and feel unable to cope with many challenges in life.

Where does this inferiority complex come from? How does it develop? For Adler, several sources of inferiority complex seemed most plausible, all rooted in childhood experience. The following are three possible examples illustrating the formation of inferiority complexes. As a child, an individual has a severe physical illness that prevents normal functioning. Adler called this *organ inferiority*. Adler believed the individual's illness would shape the personality attempting to overcome this deficit. If resolution was unsuccessful, the person developed an inferiority complex.

A second source of inferiority is rooted in the parent-child relationship. Adler felt that pampering was the most serious parental error; the parents give the child too much attention and are over-protective. This robs the child of independence. Thus, the child feels he or she is the most important person in the world. When the child leaves the home to go to school, the child discovers he or she is not the center of attention. This comes as a shock. The child had never had to solve personal problems or wait for anything — the child has little *social tolerance*. Adler believed that this would lead the child to think there is something wrong with him or her, but the real problem is the lack of social training. This can result in an inferiority complex.

A third possible source of inferiority comes from another poor parenting practice, namely neglect. A child who is rejected lacks love and support, has poor boundaries, and little guidance may internalize these problems feeling that there is something wrong with him or her, but never knowing the exact nature of the problem nor how to fix it. Thus, the individual grows up angry, distrustful, cold, and distant. As an adult, this person may have problems developing strong interpersonal relationships due to an overwhelming sense of inferiority.

Ultimate Goal of Striving

Striving for superiority is the ultimate goal of striving to overcome feelings of inferiority. Individuals are not trying to be better than everyone else. Rather, they strive for superiority in an effort to attain a sense of personal fulfilment. An individual uses his or her dissatisfaction in failing at superiority as a motivator to attain a sense of personal fulfilment. An individual's dissatisfaction with present abilities drives one to develop and further enhance those abilities. Feelings of inferiority can be constructive or destructive. These feelings are constructive when one attempts to compensate for them in ways that are healthy. They are destructive if they intensify and become overwhelming so that the person gives up. They can also be destructive if one dwells on them, but does not give up, leading to overcompensation (i.e., superiority complex).

Social interest was Adler's term encompassing the notion that everyone is born with an innate potential and motivation to co-operate with others and achieve not only their own goals, but social goals that benefit more generally without any obvious direct benefit to the individual. A "mature" individual would possess a high degree of social interest. As Dreikurs (1973, 20) explains:

> The normal individual has an optimum amount of social interest. Even when he has a goal of superiority, it still includes the welfare of others. His goal of superiority is less accentuated, less dogmatized. The motivation of the neurotic stems from his greater inferiority feelings.

Normal development was marked by unimpaired maturation throughout one's life. Conversely, neurosis is marked by the impaired ability to mature. "Neurosis is the sclerosis (hardening) of the mind; it is what impairs the process of maturation" (Krausz 1973, 53). The degree of social interest a person possessed was displayed through one of several basic lifestyles (described in the next section). Current Adlerian authorities render *social interest* as *community feeling* as the more accurate translation of the German term. See Slavik & Croake (1999) and Ferguson-Dreikurs (1995).[1] After Adler returned to Austria from service in World War I, the concept of social interest became paramount in Adler's theory of personality, even superceding the importance of the ever-present driving force of inferiority feelings.

Whereas Freud taught that behaviour was determined by the past (i.e., childhood experiences), Adler taught that behaviour was determined by the goals one sets for the future. For Adler, the ultimate goal of this striving was an ideal or finalism commonly termed *fictional finalism.* In life, many goals are potentialities and not actualities; they are not tangible. Even in a society in general, most of what we strive for are ideals (e.g., a society where all people are equal, a society with no homelessness). These ideals, although they do not fit reality, are used to guide daily living. As an example, consider Christianity. Many Christians believe that if they behave in a certain way, they will get to heaven. There is no direct evidence that heaven exists, but they act as if it exists. Adler would argue that what matters is the belief and how it guides behaviour (i.e., one's interpretation of reality that leads to maturity or social interest). All psychological processes (i.e., lifestyles) are fixed on attaining this goal. Therefore, it is perhaps, more accurate to say that while the ultimate goal of striving is for superiority (which is spurred by feelings of inferiority), this superiority is really a fictional view of how the individual can best contribute to society (social interest). Thus, one can begin to understand how Adler came to see social interest as the cardinal facet in his personality theory.

Although not totally obvious to most readers, Adler's theory deals with the past, present, and future simultaneously. All behaviours, thought processes, and attitudes are shaped by past experiences which lead to habits, heuristics for dealing with situations. The mature individual has the ability to evaluate present situations without automatically applying past solutions (i.e., falling into old habits). In short, the individual has free will,

---

1. Further, W B Wolfe, translator of Adler's (1954) *Understanding Human Nature,* writes: "The word 'Gemeinschaftsgefühl' for which no adequate English equivalent exists, has been rendered as 'social feeling' throughout the book. 'Gemeinschaftsgefühl' however connotes the sense of human solidarity, the connectedness of man to man in a cosmic relationship. Wherever the brief phrase 'social feeling' has been used therefore the wider connotation of a 'sense of fellowship in the human community' should be borne in mind.

the freedom to choose a course of action in response to a stimulus. Everyone is driven by a fictional view of the future, a future that individuals would like to make reality. The actions of the individual in the present can bring one closer to realizing that future if one is wise. Thus, at any given time, three simultaneous forces (i.e., past experience, present situation, future goals) exert pressure on the individual.

A person is best interpreted in terms of what the individual *wants* rather than what the individual *is*. That is to say, strategies (i.e., habits, lifestyle) can be changed and those changes will be logically consistent with attaining the fictional finalism in question. For example, if what a mature individual wants in the future can be accomplished by applying old principles or solutions, so be it. However, if those methods are evaluated as insufficient, the mature individual can (with training) "unlearn" these solutions in order to apply more useful solutions which may lead one closer to the finalism envisioned by that individual. The "solutions" referred to here are typified by the individual's style of life.

Lifestyles: Overcoming Feelings of Inferiority

Individuals want to attain their ultimate goal of superiority or personal perfection so they can contribute to society in a meaningful way (i.e., social interest). Adler claimed that individuals express this striving for superiority in their own unique way, called the *style of life*, also referred to as *lifestyle*. Lifestyles consist of both concerns over inferiority and the patterns of behaviour an individual develops to deal with these feelings in his or her striving for superiority. In attempting to overcome feelings of inferiority, individuals develop patterns typifying their style of life, formed and shaped by their social interactions and experience. One's lifestyle is typically set by about age five and is very hard to change thereafter.

Adler believed in the *creative power of the self*, claiming that everyone has the ability to create his or her own lifestyle. Individuals are not passively shaped by their experiences. They are full participants, able to make decisions and change directions. It is not the actual experience, but how one interprets and deals with it that matters. Of course, humans are creatures of habit and once they find a typical behaviour pattern (i.e. lifestyle) that works for them across a variety of situations, they tend to stick with it.

Ultimately, overcoming feelings of inferiority in a psychologically healthy manner requires a balance between striving for superiority and acknowledging one's limits. That is, knowing when to charge and attack obstacles, overcoming them so that one may lead a more productive life or knowing when an obstacle is too great, acknowledging one's limitations and setting more realistic goals. However, there are maladaptive ways to compensate for feelings of inferiority. Overcompensation occurs from trying to make up for weaknesses. This leads to a *superiority complex,* typified by an exaggerated sense of self. Such individuals can feel overly self-satisfied displaying an air of arrogance or pretentiousness. Another possible result of overcompensation is that these individuals may feel a need to work extra hard to outshine those around them. Just as maladaptive as overcompensation, some individuals may simply give up thereby overcoming an inferiority complex. Sometimes problems are so overwhelming that an individual stops trying in order to avoid feelings of failure and inferiority. These people may become reclusive, avoiding confrontations of any type and may seek to share in the glory of others to bolster their self-esteem.

The *dominant/ruling type* of person has a personality that is considered by most as assertive, even aggressive. Such individuals have little social awareness or regard for others. Their striving for superiority is so intense that they would exploit or otherwise harm others to achieve their goals. In terms of modern psychological disorders, individuals at the extreme end of this type might be diagnosed with antisocial personality disorder; sadistic persons and psychopaths also fit this type.

The *getting type* is perhaps the most common. These individuals expect to receive satisfaction from others; they expect others to please them. People are seen as valuable only as they are useful to the getting-type person. Pampered people may well end up as getting types. In terms of psychological disorders, individuals at the extreme end of this type might be diagnosed with narcissistic, borderline, or dependent personality disorders.

The *avoiding type* of person makes no attempts to deal with or face up to life's problems. These people had inferiority feelings so intense that they gave up. They are self-absorbed and somewhat fearful. Again, in terms of psychological disorders, individuals at the extreme end of this type might be diagnosed with schizoid, dependent, or even schizotypal personality disorders.

Finally, with the *socially useful type*, these individuals probably grew up in a family where the family shared, was respectful, and helpful, and did not use aggression to solve problems. As a result, as an adult, this type of person's lifestyle will reflect these conditions. This is the most desirable (i.e., psychologically healthy) resolution to the inferiority complex. These people can deal with life's problems and are altruistic.

Birth Order and the Development of Lifestyles

Adler taught that one's order of birth creates different conditions of childhood and this has an important role to play in development. Since each child is treated differently, this leads to different personalities and choices of lifestyles. It should be noted that Adler was not suggesting that birth order was the determinant of personality or the lifestyle one later developed. Rather, lifestyle is a function of birth order and there are other factors to consider as well.

The *first-born* is in a unique and enviable situation. Usually, parents are quite proud of this child and he or she receives the parents' constant, instant, and undivided attention. First-born individuals tend to be adult-oriented becoming quite responsible at a young age. As well, they commonly excel intellectually which is usually reflected in their good grades at school. However, the first-born is vulnerable to being dethroned. When the second-born child arrives, the first-born is no longer the center of attention. The first-born child will try to recapture the position of power and privilege. Those that have been excessively pampered will especially feel this. As well, the age of the child when the second-born comes along is significant. The older the first-born is before the sibling's birth, the less affected he or she will be. The child may strike out in anger (e.g., not eating, temper tantrums). When this is returned only by the parents' striking back (e.g., reprimands, punishments), the first-born comes to hate the second-born. First-born children are orientated towards the past, are nostalgic, and apprehensive about the future. This comes from a tendency to remember the "good old days" before the birth of the second-born child. They remain concerned with trying to regain the position of power. They try to exert this power over the younger child, but more is expected of them from the parents. They have an interest in maintaining order and authority and may be good organizers.

The *second-born* child is also in an unique position. The second-born child never experiences the position of power that a first-born experiences. So, if another child is born, the second-born child will not feel dethroned. Parents tend to take a much more relaxed approach to the second-born child. The second-born is in a more favourable position because the pace has already been set the second-born has a model to follow (i.e., "hit the ground running"). Competition with the first born stimulates the second-born to develop at a more rapid pace (i.e., trying to catch up to the first-born). Second-born children are not as concerned with power and are more optimistic about the future. Because the second-born is always trying to outdo the first-born, but the first-born always remains a little bit ahead, a second-born child will develop feelings of inferiority. Thus, there is a constant striving for superiority. This can work to their advantage if the striving leads to favourable results (e.g., getting good grades, playing on a sports team, becoming a doctor). However, the second-born may give up trying because he or she will never do as well as the first-born (e.g., the older sibling is always first in class, is the star athlete, is chief psychiatrist at the hospital). For this child, competition would not become part of his or her lifestyle.

For Adler, being the *youngest-born* child was the worst birth order. On a positive note, the youngest-born never gets dethroned. The youngest-born child has many pacesetters and develops at a fast pace. These children can become high achievers if the necessary compensatory mode is healthy competition. On the negative side, the youngest-born is in danger of being spoiled and never learning to do things without help. The youngest-born child becomes the "pet" of the family. This undermines the child's self-determination to strive. Sometimes the youngest-born compensates for this by striking out on a totally different path from that of his or her siblings (e.g., becoming an artist when all the other siblings are interested in law, business, and medicine). Without some type of compensatory mode of adjustment for being spoiled their entire lives, youngest-born children may retain a dependency on the family and find it hard to adjust to independent adult life.

Unique and perhaps rarest of all is the *only child*. The only child never loses the position of power and is never dethroned. They are more likely to experience stress when they are in situations where they discover they are not the center of attention. If not shown enough attention, they may be keenly disappointed. Adler taught that only children were the least likely to develop a true sense of community feeling (social interest). Rather, they would tend to use others and expect them to attend to their needs. They are often affectionate, but only insofar as it allows them to continue as the center of attention. On a more positive note, if the only child could avoid the many aforementioned pitfalls, the only child could possibly develop a strong social interest. Because only children spend more time in the company of adults, they tend to mature faster. Therefore, their peers may look to them as leaders simultaneously giving the only child the attention he or she seeks, but also giving the first born a sense of responsibility. This responsibility helps focus their efforts in a positive direction that they would not otherwise have. As well, the extra attention only children receive from their parents facilitates learning and general intellectual abilities (similar to first-born children) which is usually reflected in good scholastic performance. Alfred Adler's own life is a ready-made example of theory put into practice. When formulating his theory of personality, Adler drew extensively from his own life experiences. The reader may have noticed that many of the concepts mentioned earlier in this chapter fit aspects of Adler's life perfectly and it may have helped him tie all these concepts together.

The next three chapters develop in detail some of Adler's principles as they are applied in religious and theological contexts. Of necessity, the investigation is narrower than the introductory treatment of Adler's life.

CHAPTER 3

INDIVIDUAL PSYCHOLOGY AND PASTORAL THEOLOGY

Alfred Adler's Individual Psychology facilitates pastoral theological understanding. Specifically, faith, hope and charity as pastoral virtues may be advantageously understood within Adler's community feeling. Most Christian theologians accept that the theological virtues are supernatural gifts. Adler believed that all virtues, not being supernatural gifts, could be taught. Certain scholastic theologians believed that virtue, which does not extend beyond the capacity of the natural, could be acquired by habitual acts, a form of self-teaching. See the *Summa Theologica* Pt. I-II, Q. 63, art.3. Adler understands faith, hope and charity as arising in the natural order from an experience of community feeling.

Adler's psychological premises, like the premises in most of the modern psychologies, are negative with the exception of community feeling. Speber (1974, 56) writes: "I venture to assert that all the premises of Adler's systems are negative. The one exception is the role assigned in individual psychology to social interest." Individual Psychology emphasizes the positive aspect of a Adler's cognitive pastoral approach. Further, Speber (1974, 110) writes:

> Alfred Adler's great faith in man grew out of his conviction that human social failure was primarily due to man's not having learned to behave in a communal fashion. He firmly believed that one could *teach* virtue and methodically train people in communal feeling. In a word, Adler believed that one could promote socially useful behaviour by convincing people that it best served their own interests.

Adler expected that social interest would single-handedly change the relation of the individual to himself and others in the direction of social utility and active solidarity.

Clinebell (1979, 182) lists, in tabular form, the Traditional Therapies that are negative (i.e. focus on repair of damage) and the Growth/ Counselling Therapies, that are positive.

Table

Traditional Therapies Based on the pathology model	**Growth Counselling/Therapy** Based on the growth model.
Their primary goal is to repair personality pathology to enable the person to cope effectively with life.	The primary goal is facilitating the maximum development of potentials through the life cycle.
Focus mainly on problems, weaknesses, failures, conflicts, and pathology, and especially as these are related to unconscious processes and repression.	Focuses primary attention on strengths, assets, and potentialities; views, failures, trappedness, "sickness" in the wider context of wholeness.
Define *health* as the *absence* of gross pathology or maladaptive behaviour, and the ability of the ego to cope with inner and outer reality.	Defines *health* as the increasing use of one's potentialities, the *presence* of a high degree of unfolding wholeness.
View personal and relationship problems as caused by such factors as childhood trauma, neurotic processes, and blocked psychosexual development.	Views personal and relationship problems as symptoms of unlived life, diminished use of one's potentialities, blocked growth, and faulty learning. Pathological symptoms diminished as people grow.

Table (continued)

Traditional Therapies Based on the pathology model	Growth Counselling/Therapy Based on the growth model.
Understand people as pushed to change by the pain of the "pathology" of fixated development in the past.	Understands people as also pulled to change by their need to grow and their hope for a more fulfilled life in the future.
View people as determined, to a greater or lesser degree, by their past experiences and relationships.	Views people as capable, to an appreciable degree, of intentionally changing obsolete or destructive feelings and behaviour from the past, and of developing a more constructive life in the present and future.
Focus change efforts primarily within the psyche of individuals or, at the most, within their relationships.	Focuses change efforts in all 6 of the interdependent dimensions of a person's life and relationships and on the wider social systems that diminish or enable growth in one's community and culture.
Focus primary therapeutic attention on the unconscious aspects of the psyche.	Focuses on all levels of the psyche, conscious and unconscious.
Aim primarily at achieving insight and thus changing destructive attitudes, feelings, and self-concepts with the assumption that behavioural change will follow.	Aims at direct change of growth-diminishing attitudes, feelings, and self-concepts on the one hand, and growth-diminishing behaviour patterns on the other.

Table (continued)

Traditional Therapies Based on the pathology model	Growth Counselling/Therapy Based on the growth model.
Tend to see new developmental stages primarily in terms of new problems to be solved, complicated by unresolved problems from the past.	Sees each development stage as a new set of problems *and* possibilities for growth.
See crises mainly as traumas, problems, or stress periods (which revive old unresolved problems) with which persons must cope.	Sees crises as challenges that confront us with both the need and the opportunity to develop new strengths and learn new skills for living constructively.
Have tended to remain strongly male-orientated and to define growth in "male" ways that restrict wholeness for both women and men.	Seeks to utilize insights from feminist psychologists and therapists to facilitate androgynous wholeness in women and men.
Have tended to see spiritual growth as either irrelevant to or as derived from emotional and interpersonal growth.	Sees spiritual growth as a central, enabling dynamic in all areas of a person's growth.
The process usually involves long-term depth analysis of the psychological factors from the past seen as causing the fixation of development and the present problems.	The process of therapy involves working in many dimensions of a person's life, using a variety of action-orientated, shorter-term, integrative methods focusing more on the present and future than on the past.

Table (continued)

Traditional Therapies Based on the pathology model	Growth Counselling/Therapy Based on the growth model.
The counsellor-therapist tends to be seen as an "expert" authority-figure on the hierarchical doctor-patient model.	Focus on facilitating growth in both those whose development is severely diminished and in those who wish to increase their already appreciable effectiveness in living.
Focus mainly on helping those who have major problems in living and relating.	The counsellor-therapist is seen as a skilled guide and coach for one's growth journey, a person who also needs to continue growing. Mutual growth work among peers is encouraged.

Many individuals sense that habits of thought, practices and beliefs that were fruitful in the past are no longer useful today. This is a healthy development. Today, in keeping with the general thrust of all living communities striving and developing to meet the needs of current conditions, many Christians are reflecting on their contemporary experience, interpreting and adjusting their behaviour accordingly.

Something called "grass roots" theology is being undertaken by many theologians. By that is meant a type of theological thinking that arises out of the primary experience in life. Grass roots theology is an existential, not theoretical, theology that moves from practice to principle. However, the classical western pattern of theological understanding has been to move from principle to practice subsequently verified by reason. In grass roots theology, one moves from experience to reflection from which follows a statement of principle. Christian and non-believer alike express in their lives existential values recognized as faith, hope and charity. Dissatisfaction with classical philosophical thought as the basis for a pastoral theology often prompts theologians to seek an alternative discipline to interpret their experience. Often the alternative discipline is psychology. The shift from philosophy to psychology as an interpretive tool is more easily seen in pastoral theology than speculative theology.

Discussing the need for a "new" philosophy in order to interpret satisfactorily the thinking of Vatican II, Kobler (2000, 90) writes that "after the 1920s the quest for meaning received a more precise formulation from *phenomenology*....The first leaders here were Edmund Husserl, Max Scheler, and Martin Heidegger." Adlerian psychological understanding is a phenomenological philosophy.

Mairet understands Adler's psychology as a positive attempt at restructuring society. From a phenomenological psychological perspective the theologian is able to discern a spiritual meaning arising out of human experience. Mairet (1930, 14) says:

> What Adler proposes is not the universal study of psycho-pathology, but the practical reform of society and culture in accordance with a positive and scientific psychology to which he has contributed the first principles.

Ferguson-Dreikurs (1995, 30) notes the educational aspect of Adler's thought that assists in practical reform.

> Because Adler viewed psychopathology in terms of mistaken attitudes and beliefs, he considered therapy and counselling to be a form of education, one that helps the person learn new attitudes and beliefs....Through re-education, the individual in psychotherapy and counselling learns to have new concepts about himself and other persons....As a result of encouragement, he learns to believe that by means of his own strength and creativeness he can participate and contribute, and that he can live a more satisfying and full life.

This notion of re-education is expressed by Charles Davis, the theologian, who notes that with a new attitude the individual can direct the process of becoming a free person by setting goals where earlier mistakes were made. Davis (1967, 193) understands the re-education process as a form of cognitive therapy and writes: "At some point the individual directs the process of becoming a free man; sets goals; begins to make himself; does this in a restricted context where he has made earlier mistakes."

Adler's contribution to the educational aspect of pastoral theology is by way of his cognitive therapy that enables an individual to strive for a fulfilled and integrated life. Fulfilment or wholesome integration into a community is accomplished by setting appropriate goals and attaining them. Wholesome integration of the individual in community has been an historical concern of Jewish and Christian thinkers. This concern for wholesome integration is not exclusive to Judaism or Christianity. Other religious traditions have a similar history of concern. However, the purpose here is to focus on the individual who strives to live the Christian virtues of faith, hope and charity, with the help of an Adlerian cognitive therapy. Faith, hope and charity, the theological virtues revealed within the Christian tradition are to be theologically distinguished from similar notions arising in Adler's understanding of community feeling.

This investigation is not meant to be an historical criticism or an evaluation of the virtues of faith, hope or charity. Rather, readers are invited to assess our comments and decide to what degree what is said here coincides with their own experience and thinking. The reader's personal experience in life will play a part in the usefulness of this work. Further, this investigation is not a theoretical undertaking. This investigation is based on normal religious experience. Martin Thornton takes a similar point of view in writing his reappraisal of normal religious experience Thornton (1974, 8) writes:

> But if a study of religious experience is to be meaningful it cannot be vicarious; so this book must include my experience of my God. This fits in well enough with contemporary theology, with its emphasis on the personal-existential, and yet theological writers seem reluctant to adopt this line. I think it is time somebody took the risk.

The comments and statements made in this work are not reckoned by the authors as definitive or beyond reform. Freud, in his day, was more accurate in his psychological assessment of his clients than his writings currently reflect because social interactions and relationships have changed since then. In short, the context alters the understanding and psychological understanding is always in a state of flux as it considers individuals in their changing existential situation. The authors accept that pastoral understanding is rooted in psychological understanding. The influence of psychology in pastoral theology has been addressed in many circles since the turn of the century. Current investigations contribute fresh insights into this influence. However, not all authors agree on the positive influence of psychology as the writings of some secular psychologists attest.

We have, as human agents, the capacity to determine what we will become. The future is literally in our hands as we make decisions that shape our values that in turn shape us. With this realization comes a radical new vision of the world which abandons the classical understanding of a fixed system of thinking and allows us to fashion a future which is as yet undetermined. O'Murchu (2000, 3), from a personal perspective, notes this phenomenon.

My own faith journey includes many transitions in which new ways of understanding superseded those which previously seemed unalterable or, according to official teaching, could never change and therefore should never be abandoned.

Past generations addressed the circumstances of their day to the best of their ability as they strove to accomplish their goals. Their legacy is not false. Rather, given our modern concerns and circumstances, their legacy is inadequate for us. A fulfilling lifestyle requires that past perspectives, theological and psychological, be reinterpreted in the context of contemporary experience.

A principle within Christian theological thought is that "grace builds upon nature." A variation of this principle is "grace respects psychology." Classical philosophical thought sought to explain the secular world and to understand divine revelation within a relationship of theology and grace; contemporary philosophical thought seeks to explain the secular world and to understand divine revelation in a collaborative relationship of psychology and grace. The struggle in the present time is to understand our contemporary experience and the place of revelation while not discounting the contribution of the past. This is a healthy enterprise. Often, however, this struggle ought not to be understood as a crisis to be overcome or solved in one's life. From Adler's perspective this struggle is not a crisis in the contemporary clinical sense of the term, but rather, is part of the stages of growth and development that each individual undertakes as part of a normal life.

Traditional Christianity and western social structures have often been perceived as the sole ways of interpreting experience. Often these structures are experienced as placing constraints, to varying degrees, upon individuals and the community. The legal constraints of both civil and ecclesiastical law, the social mores, formal education and traditional customs are all examples of a type of "unfreedom," if you will, under which an individual lives. With a lifting of these constraints in civil and ecclesial contexts the individual experiences a new sense of external freedom.

But along with this external freedom an internal freedom is necessary. Internal freedom means the ability to understand and execute what is necessary in the metaphysical and spiritual life of an individual. Obviously, the ability to do this will be relative to many factors ranging from one's temperament to the family and economic situation into which the individual is born.

In striving for a metaphysical and spiritual freedom an individual may embrace the virtues of faith, hope and charity as both a goal and as a means. As the constraints of traditional habits are lifted externally and internally and individuals accept responsibility in determining the outcome of their lives, the virtues of faith, hope and charity for the Christian - indeed for anyone - are disclosed as part of that individual's healthy psychological and spiritual makeup. With a republican democracy in mind, Stein (2003) writes that:

> The early American political ideal of democracy was tempered by an awareness of the role of character. The framers of the Constitution understood well that advancing the ideal of 'liberty and justice for all' requires a virtuous citizenry.

Within the Christian tradition few would contest the understanding that a virtue is a habit that makes its possessor good and the work done good. Traditionally, the theological virtues have been understood as habits whose immediate object is God who is also the motive for doing good. From a psychological perspective, however, we recognize that, both God and individuals, can be the proper object of the theological virtues. Adlerian cognitive therapy removes any narrow denominational interpretation of community and introduces a broader understanding of the human and spiritual community. This work does not negate the classical conception of the theological virtues as divine gifts; investigation of these virtues with attention to the affective and relational dimension of the individual's response is what has been undertaken.

From a cognitive therapeutic perspective, faith is an attitude, a disposition, that an individual adopts vis à vis a perceived truth. Whether this truth is real or apparent does not render the psychological experience inauthentic. Psychologically faith is understood as a response process, not as a reaction, by an individual. A response is a co-operative understanding and defined by Funk and Wagnalls (1989) as "words and acts evoked by the words or acts of another or others," whereas, reaction tends to lack co-operation and is defined as a "tendency toward a former or reversed state of things; especially, a trend toward an earlier social, political or economic policy or condition." The notion of hope arises from an existential experience of an individual whose vision and action are directed to the future. In such a disposition there is an expectation on the part of the individual that the future holds some form of goodness, of blessedness, that is in fact attainable although this may be difficult. Process and orientation in the present moment provide the context of the virtue of hope. Charity is that emotive feeling (movement) that is evoked by another. Love of one's fellows and charity are virtually identical. The scholastics distinguished between natural love and supernatural love (that is, good willed to oneself or another for God's sake).

We are not the first, nor indeed the last to recognize that classical philosophy is no longer adequate for the interpretation of contemporary experience. William James, in the preface of his work, *Varieties of Religious Experience*, admits the same. He attempted to show the adequacy of philosophy in satisfying religious interpretation of experience. However, what he realized was that psychology was better suited to the task.

In many ways James has presented ideas and conclusions that are similar to those of Adler. Like cognitive therapists today, James observed that the affective experience is often more powerful than the actual event. Adler agrees, given his use of a psychological fiction which attempts to help the individual strive for a healthy lifestyle. Whether or not the psychological fiction corresponds to a reality is secondary in Adler's thought. Likewise, James refers to a special reality that is not perceived through our ordinary senses but conceived "as if" that reality existed. This notion of "as if" is tantamount to Adler's psychological fiction. The "as if" notion is given a thorough philosophical treatment by Vaihinger (1952).

In his lectures, James (1908) uses two significant terms. One term is "mind-cure" and the other is "faith-state." A healthy mindedness is necessary for a healthy religious experience. He states in Lectures IV and V that "mind-cure" is described as an optimistic scheme of life. He considers the large group of individuals striving to achieve this positive attitude worth studying as a psychic group. Further, he acknowledges that both Catholics and Protestants have sincere exponents in the "mind-cure" movement who have more in common than they first may realize.

"Faith-state" is a term that James discovered in Professor Leuba's writings. James accepts the definition given by Leuba but prefers to employ the term, "state of assurance." Should one attain this state of assurance three psychological characteristics become evident. These are: i) a loss of all worry or anxiety, ii) a perception of truths not known before, iii) and an apparent change in the objective appearance of the world (James 1908, 248). Adler recognizes these states as symptoms indicative of a life-style of an individual who has attained a higher degree of community feeling. James accepts that individuals can achieve unity with something greater than themselves. It is within this unity that humans find great peace. This is similar to Adler's understanding of one of the purposes of religion. Indeed, it is one of the things that religion does best for the individual, according to Adler.

There are a number of cognitive therapeutic theories about the person in vogue today. Some are more suitable than others in investigating the psychological makeup of an individual from a theological point of view. Freud, Jung, Erikson, Maslow and others have broken ground here and have given us new insights into the relationship between cognitive therapy and pastoral theology. Slavik (2000, 39) develops Adler's understanding of the person as the "active element in the social field, the entity that interacts meaningfully in the field with others." Adler introduced a system of cognitive therapy that reflects a holistic and humanistic understanding of the human condition that stresses the importance of the individual being positively nurtured within the environment. The purpose of his system is to enable those emotionally disabled to become useful and an asset to society. Cognitive therapy discloses spiritual activity as a psychological activity of the individual. Through spiritual activity the individual strives towards community goals and values. Individuals live in a social context and express their belief and faith religiously within that social context. This is done with varying degrees of intensity.

Individual Psychology is not interested in the verbal expression of feelings, but only in the intensity of a person's movement. Therefore it will not be able to evaluate the representatives of various religions by the way they express their feelings, but only by their movements as whole individuals, i.e., by their fruits. These fruits must, of course, be recognized *sub specie aeternitatis* (under the aspect of eternity). (Adler 1964, 283)

Adlerian psychology contains diverse principles and it is difficult to present a systematic body of this thought. However, principles recognized by Adler through his cognitive therapy can be extended and applied in understanding the Christian experience. These principles shed light on the human psyche and serve in clarifying the behaviour of religious individuals. Investigating the suitability of Adler's Individual Psychology has taken up the first part of this work. Now follows a deeper consideration of the relationship between cognitive therapy and pastoral theology.

CHAPTER 4

COGNITIVE THERAPY AND PASTORAL THEOLOGY

Cognitive therapy and pastoral theology are differing forms of knowledge and understanding but they share a number of characteristics in common. First, both have many proponents with diverse points of view. There are schools of pastoral theology just as there are schools of cognitive therapy. Secondly, pastoral theology arises out of earlier theological ways of thinking just as cognitive therapy arises out of previous psychological ways of thinking. Brian Gaybba speaks of a monastic school of theology in contrast to a scholastic school of theology. Gaybba (1988, 1) writes that prior to Bonaventure (1221-1274) and Aquinas (1225-1274) "theology as a body of knowledge was equated with the contents of scripture. The situation changed dramatically when theology was seen as a body of knowledge resulting from human reflection on scripture." The historical social conditions under which theologians reflect and write influence their understanding and interpretation of those events. As a case in point, Martin Thornton gives the subtitle, "An outline of ascetical theology according to the English pastoral tradition," to his book *English Spirituality*. Thornton (1963, 55), explains that

> a large part of ascetical theology consists in adapting dogmatic truth to the needs of different temperaments....'The English Temperament' obviously embraces enormous diversity...yet the English temperament remains a recognizable entity, bearing on the development of our spirituality.

Thirdly, theologians and cognitive therapists have seen fit to alter their understanding within their respective disciplines in light of new knowledge. William McDougall's psychological thinking presents a shift from an intellectual understanding to a hormic one. McDougall (1930, 28) notes:

> The hormic theory is radically opposed to intellectualism and all its errors, the errors that have been the chief bane of psychology (and of European culture in general) all down the ages. It does not set out with some analytic description of purely cognitive experience, and then find itself at a loss for any intelligible functional relation between this and bodily activities. It recognizes fully the conative nature of all activity and regards the cognitive power as everywhere the servant and the guide of striving. Thus it is fundamentally dynamic and leads to a psychology well adapted for application to the sciences and practical problems of human life, those of education, of hygiene, of therapy, of social activity, of religion, of mythology, of aesthetics of economics, of politics and the rest.

The shift away from intellectual thinking occurring in both disciplines serves to aid the individual in understanding experience. Adler's (1943, 277) Individual Psychology recognizes this.

> If I am venturing now to maintain the right of Individual Psychology to be accepted as a view of the universe, since I use it for the purpose of explaining the meaning of life, I have to exclude all moral and religious conceptions that judge between virtue and vice. I do this although I have been convinced for a long time that both ethics and religion as well as political movements have continually aimed at doing justice to the meaning of life and that they have developed under the pressure of social feeling, which is an absolute truth. ....
> According to this position every tendency should be reckoned as justified whose direction gives undeniable proof that it is guided by the goal of universal welfare. Every tenet should be held to be wrong if it is opposed to this standpoint or is vitiated by the query of Cain: "Am I my brother's keeper?"

As distinct disciplines, psychology and theology are often not easily integrated. In the minds of many they are in fact at cross purposes. Much has changed and in present times theologians and psychologists have become aware of their interdependence.

Alexander Müller (1992) a close associate of Adler, wrote *You Shall Be a Blessing* which presents a case in point of the psychologist - theologian relationship.

In contemporary theological thinking pastoral theology is distinguished from systematic theology by virtue of the philosophical perspective adopted. Within the Roman tradition, it was with the Second Vatican

Council that pastoral theology began to make great strides in application and development. Some commentators noted with optimism that in its deliberations the Council's purpose was intentionally pastoral, not doctrinal (systematic). Austin Flannery (1996, 172) appends a note to his translation of the Council's document, *Gaudium et Spes*. "The constitution is called 'pastoral' because, while resting on doctrinal principles, it sets out the relation of the Church to the world and to the people of today." The Council's theologians were allowed and encouraged, to some degree, to seek in secular studies and disciplines that which is positive and supportive of an individual's development and growth as a human being. John Kobler (2000) recognizes the Council's intent and calls for a phenomenological philosophy, not a speculative philosophy, to be given serious consideration in interpreting the mind of the Second Vatican Council.

The purpose of cognitive therapy is the betterment of the individual. On an individual and collective basis the well-being of the person is desired. It is in their praxis that a cognitive therapy and a pastoral theology overlap and in fact are complementary. What needs to be distinguished is the way in which each assists the individual in striving for a healthy and fulfilling life. Adler (1931, 12) phrases it: "We approach the problem from a different angle, but the goal is the same -- to increase interest in others."

Indeed, for the cognitive therapist all humanistic religions offer some betterment of persons in the context of their life situation. In the many forms of humanistic religious activity and in the world's great revealed faiths of Judaism, Christianity and Islam, cognitive therapists recognize the common factor of the betterment of the person in community. Further, much pastoral theology, in its contemporary understanding, takes into account the non-Christian experience. Wilfrid Smith's (1982, 9) observations are of value.

> The time will soon be with us when a theologian who attempts to work out his position unaware that he does so as a member of a world society in which other theologians equally intelligent, equally devout, equally moral, are Hindus, Buddhists, Muslims, and unaware that his readers are likely perhaps to be Buddhists or to have Muslim husbands or Hindu colleagues - such a theologian is as out of date as is one who attempts to construct an intellectual position unaware that Aristotle has thought about the world or that existentialists have raised new orientations, or unaware that the earth is a minor planet in a galaxy that is vast only by terrestrial standards.

The Second Vatican Council (Flannery 1996, 570) affirms in its Declaration of the Relation of the Church to Non-Christian Religions that the Catholic Church rejects nothing of what is true and holy in these religions. It has a high regard for the manner of life and conduct, the precepts and doctrines which, although differing in many ways from its own teaching, nevertheless often reflect a ray of that truth which enlightens all men and women.

Can the activity of the cognitive therapist and the pastoral theologian be compared? Each seeks to enable the individual to achieve some degree of health in life. Each seeks to promote the welfare of the individual and the community. Each undertakes differing approaches in striving for what is recognized as a common goal. In striving towards this goal often psychological and theological purposes cross and principles common to pastoral theologians and cognitive therapists can be applied.

The varying points of view among the schools of theology and psychology, including Adlerian psychology, testify that rigidity and complacency are to be avoided. It is in the area of pastoral understanding and cognitive therapy that theology and psychology can be of mutual assistance. Psychology, being the more recent discipline, can learn much from theology by integrating the understanding of various spiritual traditions. Theology can profit greatly from psychology's contribution to the understanding of the human existential response.

In pastoral theology, growth and development are matters of spiritual direction. Growth and development are activities that are natural to the individual. Growth may be understood from both a psychological and theological perspective. The individual member of the human race, theologically or psychologically considered, is not a static being. Spiritual direction takes many forms. It may consist of formal and systematic investigations of life, or of the acceptance of some viewpoint offered by a mentor, or of a more general approach to the everyday regulation of interpersonal relationships.

From a classical theological perspective the goal of spiritual direction is perfection. In the contemporary context the notions perfection and spiritual direction are often misunderstood. Perfection does not mean an absence of error or to be without flaw. This is a contemporary understanding of the word not found in the spiritual traditions of pre-modern times. Rather, it is a recognition that all the knowledge and understanding as necessary means, inadequate as they are to strive for a goal, are available to the individual in this life. The ascetical theologian Adolphe Tanquery (1930, 156), in his treatise on the spiritual life, discusses a *relative* perfection. He notes that *relative* perfection is also *progressive* and "consists in the approach toward that end [goal] by the development of all one's faculties and the carrying out in practice of all duties, in accordance with the dictates of the natural law as manifested by right reason." Striving for perfection develops the understanding of *Gemeinschaftsgefühl* and enables the individual to bring it to fruition. The goal of relative perfection can be achieved, on earth, insofar as the human condition permits. It is never achieved fully.

As well, the term spiritual direction is not to be understood as "pastoral counselling" with an emphasis on the clinical aspect dealing with the immediate troubling issues of a practical life. Martin Thornton (1959, 43) notes:

> I do not wish to attack brothers in Christ who are doing charitable work, nor to enter into a pedantic quibble over words. The fact remains that, to the uninitiated, 'pastoral counselling' sounds very much as if it ought to be spiritual direction; guidance in prayer, over a long period, positive, and based entirely on ascetical and moral theology: which is exactly what it is not. It would be quite dreadful if a Christian who really wanted direction presented himself for 'counselling.'

According to the spiritual tradition followed, there is more than one means to reach perfection. Striving for perfection is a continuous process as Thornton (1963, 23) notes.

Christian theology interprets life through two domains. Each affects the individual's spiritual life. One is the world of human experience *a parte Dei* and the other is the world of human experience *a parte hominibus*. Each is understood differently by the Christian. The spiritual life, *a parte Dei,* leads to an attitude of *Gemeinschaftsgefühl* through a theological understanding. The other, *a parte hominibus,* leads to *Gemeinschaftsgefühl* a psychic attitude that relates to the quality of life and social feeling. Of this social feeling Adler (Ansbacher & Ansbacher 1956, 135) says,

> When we say it is a feeling, we are certainly justified in doing so. But it is more than a feeling; it is an evaluative attitude toward life (*Lebensform*). .... We are not in a position to define it quite unequivocally, but we have found in an English author a phrase which clearly expresses what we could contribute to an explanation: 'To see with the eyes of another, to hear with the ears of another, to feel with the heart of another.' For the time being, this seems to me an admissible definition of what we call social feeling.

Christian spiritual direction engages the unique understanding of social feeling *a parte Dei.* The believer understands that God, in Christ, takes the initiative and that the believer's part is to respond. Western spiritual masters have developed this understanding through the centuries. There is a curriculum in the spiritual life that both the director and the disciple are obliged to follow. Whether the director is God, or a spiritual master, the disciple's role is to respond. In Hughson's (1950, 24) words: "In this curriculum two basic things are necessary: first there must be grace and power from God; and second, there must be steadfast co-operation by us with what God is seeking to do in our soul."

Accounting for God's initiative belongs to speculative theology which is a discipline in its own right. Quoting Dr. Mascall, Martin Thornton (1959, 8) notes

> that what a being *is* precedes what it *does; our actions are a consequence of what we are....*It will follow from this that the Christian should be defined not in terms of what he himself does, but of what God has made him to be. Being a Christian is an ontological fact, resulting from an act of God.

This Christian understanding does not derive from immediate experience but rather from reflection on the experience in the world that is proper to existential theology. Thornton's form of existential understanding needs to be distinguished from that of Kierkegaard, Heidegger, Sartre, Camus and Anouilh. The existential observation made by Hughson (1950, 24) in his study of human destiny is significant and similar to Thornton's understanding. "Let us, then, take God's part for granted, and consider what should be done to secure our own faithfulness." Our own faithfulness can be secured through Alfred Adler's cognitive therapy as a means of developing a lifestyle and spiritual health. Adler thinks as a humanistic existentialist, *a parte hominibus.* He says: (Adler 1943, 11)

> I made it strictly my business never to make any statement I could not illustrate and prove from my own experience....I believe I am not bound by any strict rule or prepossession, but rather subscribe to the maxim: Everything can be something else as well.

Through their understanding of revelation Christians hold that it is part of God's initiative to stir up our desire for God. Others hold that this desire for a god-like goal is natural to the person - believer or otherwise - since it is innate to the natural constitution of human beings. Murry (1929, 170) writes from this perspective.

> We have now transposed the mystical experience from the supernatural order into the order of a complete naturalism....The question now arises whether the mystical certainty, thus transposed into the order of a complete naturalism, is capable to any man of honesty and good will. Have we attained

a picture of the Universe, such that it really satisfies both the demands of the mind and the desires of the heart, and by satisfying these enables an organic unity of the inward man to be established, and a unity of that organic unity with the organic unity of the Universe?

Indeed, within the universe this striving for unity, expressed through community feeling, is what distinguishes the human animal from all others. Humans are religious animals and community feeling may be expressed religiously in one's lifestyle through a co-operative and social culture. Ansbacher & Ansbacher (1956, 134) note that:

> The high degree of cooperation and social culture which man needs for his very existence demands spontaneous social effort, and the dominant purpose of education is to evoke it. Social interest is not inborn [as a full-fledged entity], but is an innate potentiality which has to be consciously developed.

The believer, however, will experience this development as a spiritual, not psychic, power in life. This power enables the believer to overcome obstacles and enables one to achieve that which is good as a goal in life. This spiritual power affects health and well-being. The non-believer will also lay claim in this life to a power that affects health. This is an existential power and is recognized in striving for a goal. This is the power of movement which Adler predicates only of humans. This power of movement is a psychic activity rather than a spiritual activity. Adler (1954, 17,18,20) understands the human soul as movement which suggests power in the psychic sense. He writes:

> We attribute a soul only to moving, living organisms. The soul stands in innate relationship to free motion....This movability stimulates, promotes, and requires an always greater intensification of the psychic life....It seems hardly possible to recognize in the psychic organ, the soul, anything but a force acting toward a goal, and Individual Psychology considers all the manifestations of the human soul as though they were directed toward a goal.

The following understanding of power from the perspective of pastoral theology, offered by Hughson (1950, 96), is useful since it defines the goal (purpose) of a virtue. "Power may be defined as the possession of a right, ability and freedom to act with efficiency in some given sphere in relation to a definite objective."

Christians understand the virtues of faith, hope and charity as powers or spiritual movement developed within the ascetical life in relation to a definite objective (goal). Tanquery (1930, 550), like Thomas Aquinas, writes of these particular virtues as theological. "Here on earth, charity always includes the other two theological virtues. It is, so to speak, their *soul,* their *vital principle* or *life;* so much so, that, devoid of charity, faith and hope remain imperfect, inert, dead." The virtues as powers are striving to bring about some good, accomplish some beneficial end regarding the development of the person in community. St. Paul speaks of such power in I Corinthians 13. St. Paul understands that faith, hope, and charity are effective powers that bring about growth, development, and well-being in the individual. Faith brings about a relationship with truth; hope brings about an enjoyment of security, charity brings about an overcoming of evil or harmfulness that threatens to destroy or at least debilitate the individual or community.

Generally, Adlerian cognitive therapy suggests the same. That is, to strive for truth, security and health is of paramount importance to the well-being of society. Religious individuals have historically understood themselves as bearers of a moral will towards the community. Adler recognized the moral responsibility that individuals have to the community.

To understand why Adler would accept the harmonious order of truth, security and health as indicative of a healthy life-style we must remember that he, along with others of that generation, lived through a world war that was most devastating and barbaric. Due to the severity of the war he and other thinkers of the time were influenced to conceive human co-operation as necessary for the survival and the health of the human race. Graef (1959, 10) makes the observation about that era that philosophical existentialism "was admirably suited to the world of the twentieth [century] rent by total war and shaken to its foundations by dictatorships outstripping any cruelties that could be found in the pages of history books."

From an Adlerian point of view, an understanding of the person's feelings of inferiority and the corresponding goal of superiority needs to be understood simultaneously. These terms, inferiority and superiority, are not to be understood as pejorative concepts but rather as terms indicating a context or frame of reference in which an individual strives to overcome obstacles in life. Through striving to move from an inferior position (one previously accepted) to a superior position (one currently desired) one works towards a goal. Faith is part of this striving. It is through faith, an attitude seeking truth and well-being that the individual strives to participate fully in the life of the community. One's attitude within the community is indicative of one's lifestyle. Christian individuals understand their churches and fellowship groups as communities of faith moving toward well-being. The degree of expression of the theological virtues of faith, hope, and charity determines the degree of health of a Christian community.

Life is not static. Psychologists and existential theologians recognize the individual entity as a dynamic social construct. The classical understanding has been to view the good, the perfect, the virtuous as something fixed, an ideal to which one conforms. This understanding remains acceptable in some schools of thought. However, it is not a satisfactory understanding within existential pastoral theology or Adlerian cognitive therapy. The static approach is no doubt due to a persistent reliance on classical Greek thinking derived from Aristotle (384-322 BCE) and Plato (427-347 BCE). In classical Greek thinking lived experience is somehow a shadow of reality.

Dewart (1966, 134) notes the role played by *ananke* (necessity) and *moira* (fate) in Greek culture. To envision health as conforming to an ideal or fixed form is incompatible with Adlerian cognitive therapy. Adler makes the criticism that: "The human spirit is only too well accustomed to reduce everything that is in flux to a form, to consider it not as movement, but as frozen movement - movement that has become form" (Adler 1943, 269). Indeed, Adler's cognitive therapy shows that it is in the striving, the movement which advances improvement that the good is achieved fully.

Meaning in life varies from individual to individual. The meaning one gives to life may be healthy or unhealthy. This choice can be recognized from one's life-style. In a healthy individual meaning cannot be private but must be communal. In fact, private meaning is no meaning at all in Adlerian thought. Graef (1959, 17) writes: "For the atheist existentialist, the absurdity of the world is the result of logic -- *his* logic. And it is his 'morality' to go on living in this world with the full knowledge of the absurdity of life, a kind of perverted heroism." Henry (2001, 42) warns of a mistaken understanding of private meaning. He writes:

> The more profound these experiences, the less easy they are to communicate to others, and the more private and personal they become. In order for them to constitute a true picture of the inner archetypal events, and not merely to represent idiosyncrasies and half-forgotten personal experiences of some particular individual, it is necessary for them to be submitted to the censorship of the group.

Attempts believers make at a lifestyle incorporating the theological virtues must be lived out in a communal context. Such a context enables a pastoral theological interpretation that stresses the necessary relationship between the individual and the community. As the virtues are experienced individually they, in fact, become meanings for the community. Whether or not the community can share in the experiences of each member establishes the degree of unity and health of the community. Human communities, in general, are not inclined to follow neurotics with their private set of meanings. In all humanistic religious activity the goal is the same - i.e., the well-being of the community. In all religions we find this concern for the salvation of man. As Adler phrases it: "In all great movements of the world men have been striving to increase social interest, and religion is one of the greatest strivings in this way" (Adler 1931, 11).

From a psychological perspective this goal of community feeling may be understood either as a Christian notion of redemption from sin or as a cognitive therapeutic attempt at betterment. Most Adlerians recognize the cognitive therapeutic movement as a striving for the betterment of the community or *Gemeinschaftsgefühl*. Practising the virtues of faith, hope, and charity are part of the Christian religious lifestyle that strives to achieve the same goal. Since faith, hope, and charity as Christian virtues are goals indicative of a healthy individual, the lack of these virtues, is indicative of an unhealthy individual. Absence of community feeling according to Adler would indicate an unhealthy lifestyle. It may even be said to be a neurotic life-style. It is healthy for an individual to be focussed on the community and possess a goal of social welfare. Adler (1964a, 6)

For general guidance I would like to propound the following rule: *as soon as a goal of a psychic movement or its life-plan has been recognized, then we are to assume that all movements of its constituent parts will coincide with both the goal and the life-plan.*

The virtuous lifestyle is community oriented and goal directed. Incorporation of faith, hope and charity into a life plan will advance the health of society and the health of the individual. Christians, in selecting the virtues as goals, will avoid neurotic behaviour and create a healthy environment for themselves and others.

This brings us now to a detailed consideration of the theological virtues in the context of *Gemeinschaftsgefühl*.

CHAPTER 5

THE VIRTUES: FAITH, HOPE AND CHARITY

Faith

Faith is the response-movement to an invitation which presupposes a capacity to relate. God is the object of faith in the sense that recognizing God as a subject sets up a relationship between two individuals. This relationship is a dynamic one which means that it has the capacity to grow and develop. However, the act of faith proves nothing as to the existence of God. It is a subjective experience that admits of no verifiable scientific investigation. The faith response initiated by one individual inspires this same response in others of like disposition. Faith, then, has a communal dimension. Adler is working with a psychology of values which departs from the Freudian school. Adlerian cognitive therapy assists a believer in responding to God's initiative. Thus, it assists pastoral theology in striving to improve health and well-being by encouraging an individual's faith-response within the community.

God is not a pre-existent being in Adlerian thought, (this notion has been inherited from Hellenic thinking), but rather a noble idea that has appeared in human conscious expression. The notion of God arises from the natural inclination to strive for perfection that posits God as a goal. That is part of the process of striving to accomplish the betterment of the individual. Adler (1964, 275) notes:

One concretization of the idea of perfection, the highest image of greatness and superiority, which has always been very natural for man's thinking and feeling, is the contemplation of a deity. To strive towards God, to be in Him, to follow His call, to be one with Him -- from this goal of striving (not of a drive), there follow attitude, thinking, and feeling.

For the believer that goal, the idea of perfection, is God, the father of Abraham, Isaac and Jacob. The goal is an ontological reality. For the non-believer that goal may remain an ideal of perfection, a metaphysical reality. In both cases the dynamic of faith is the same. The attitude of faith is not an additive to an individual's experience. It is not acquired. It is an awareness of the faith-response that arises within the experiences of life. The faith act, in fact, characterizes one's humanity. An individual grows physically, psychologically and spiritually. Whether one is a Christian or Buddhist, or a non-believer, growth towards perfection takes place through an attitude of faith. Adler (1964, 278) accepts this when he writes:

> The strong possibilities of a concretization of a final goal of perfection and the irresistible attraction to it are firmly anchored in the nature of man, in the structure of his psychological apparatus. So, too, are the possibilities of psychological joining with others. The sanctification of these possibilities strengthened them in their development by setting the entire thinking and feeling apparatus into continuous movement.

The faith response brings about some change, movement or development in the individual. An individual who is faithful toward the person of Christ ought to be able to show signs of being a Christian, ie, being a forgiving individual, being a compassionate and generous person. The text of the Vatican Council Document on the Liturgy recognizes the dual character of faith. Faith may be understood as a gift to the individual and as a response on an individual's part. As Flannery (1975, 173) writes:

> The purpose of the Profession of Faith (or Creed) is to express the *assent* and *response* of the people to the scripture reading and homily they have just heard, and to recall to them the main truths of the faith, before they begin to celebrate the Eucharist [emphasis mine].

Christian theology teaches that God is made manifest to the believer through the written word (scripture) and through the spoken word (preaching). Therefore, it is proper to speak of a faith attitude to the word and to preaching (kerygma) which is tantamount to a relationship with God.

We must distinguish between true faith and simulated faith. How to distinguish between the two is a question of discernment and impinges on the notion of the psychological health of the individual. Individuals of true faith will recognize each other. Or, considered another way, an unhealthy individual will likely appear neurotic to the community. Faith, for Adlerians, is the affective response shown in the individual's striving for a healthy community feeling. The goal of a healthy community feeling inspires faith and in turn affects the condition of others in striving for the same goal.

Given, as Adler postulates, that the individual makes his meaning in life within a communal context, an individual striving towards a goal opposed to community feeling would be an unhealthy individual, an inauthentic individual. This would be a person simulating faith. The individual simulating faith has recognized something less than community feeling as a goal and strives for that. "In theological terms those with an inauthentic faith have confused something less than God with God" (McBrien 1987, 57).

In light of Adler's understanding it becomes increasingly difficult to articulate the view that faith is exclusively a divine gift as if it were something added to an individual nature by a external power. This, however, has been the long-held view of scholastic theologians. But not all classical theologians are in accord. Even before modern psychology made inroads into theological thought certain thinkers challenged this view. F. R. Tennant (1943, 78) writes:

> Faith is an outcome of the inborn propensity to self-conservation and self-betterment which is a part of human nature, and is no more a miraculously superadded endowment than is sensation or understanding.

This tension between the classical notion of faith and the contemporary notion is not unhealthy. Since an individual's experience varies from generation to generation and culture to culture, it is reasonable that one's faith relationship varies from generation to generation, culture to culture. This is possible because the Christian faith is not wedded to any given cultural form, any more than it is to be found as a pure essence, devoid of concrete cultural form. The Christian faith can be cast not only in the traditional concepts but also in the novel, emergent concepts that an evolving human experience creates (Dewart 1966, 118). Cognitive therapy will invite us to look to the individual's behaviour, goals and lifestyle to discover an authentic living of the virtuous life. The traditional notion of "having faith" or "not having faith" needs to be reconsidered. The psychological and theological dispositions concerning faith need to be understood from a subjective point of view. While not attempting to negate the intent of classical thought, Adler suggests that modern individuals need to recognize within themselves a dynamic that strives for the same goal that humans have held throughout time. By nature each individual possesses an innate creative power. Adler (1964, 40) writes:

> Every human being brings the disposition for social interest with him; but then it must be *developed* through *upbringing*, especially through correct guidance of the *creative power* of the individual" [Adler's italics].

However, from a theological point of view Adler did express some thoughts that were disconcerting. Although he has contributed to a better understanding of religious activity through his psychological insights, at one point in his writings he did make a prediction that scientific illumination will eventually replace religious faith. Ansbacher & Ansbacher (1956, 462) cite Adler that: "Religious faith is alive and will continue to live until it is replaced by this most profound insight and the religious feeling which stems from it. It will not be enough for man to taste of this insight; he will have to devour and digest it completely."

However, there is no malice intended here. Adler has replaced traditional understanding with principles from his own reflective thought. Hendrika Vande Kemp (1985, 141) concludes:

> Adler himself clearly regarded individual psychology as a form of, or equivalent to, religion. It was religious in that it subordinated all other efforts to the ultimate goal of ideal community and the strengthening of social interest. Thus, Adler definitely regarded psychotherapy as a religious process.

Christians understand that it is in the faith response that individuals strive towards Christian community. In this striving the Christian and the Individual Psychologist have the same goal. Jahn is correct when he classes Adler as an influential humanist and not a Christian psychologist. "Whereas Jahn claims that it is faith that urges man toward community, in Individual Psychology guidance is the deeply felt conviction that the only right way of solving human problems is that which would benefit an ideal community." (Adler 1964, 283)

Ansbacher and Ansbacher (Adler 1964, 273) note Jahn's theological perspective.

> The perspective of the psychotherapist and the view of the minister are not entirely comparable. Psychology is, as a rule, convinced that man can free himself from his conflicts, or that the psychotherapeutic treatment can do so.

According to the religious view, redemption is brought about only by the gift of grace or the gift of salvation. Luther said that the beginning of sin is pride, disregard of God, and the love of self. The greatest achievement of Individual Psychology is a similar understanding that men break down because of their demonic self-love. Adler's therapy is to bring the patient with love into society. For him the brotherhood of man is a goal of almost religious enthusiasm. While we agree with him fully with regard to the human community, we maintain that beyond this there is also an other-worldly community, the community of God, the *unio mystica*. For Adler, the meaning of life is the experience of fellowmanship and the courage for it. There are, however, human problems which can be solved neither by fellowmanship nor by courage. Furthermore, while Christianity unreservedly endorses the call for encouragement, it holds that there can be no courage for life without faith in God. And it is God who gives life its ultimate meaning. For Adler, God is a human idea; for Christians God is revealed.

We now must turn our attention to the virtue of hope and investigate its connection with faith.

Hope

Geach discusses the classical understanding of hope asserting that hope becomes specifically Christian when orientated to its object, God, in the person of Christ. "I shall try to show that any other hope, for individuals or for the human race, is quite unfounded" he states (Geach 1977, xii). This perspective reflects the understanding that Christian philosophers and theologians have had since the medieval times. Adler has presented us with the possibility of understanding our experiences, in particular our religious experiences, with a set of existential tools. However, existential thought, to the minds of some, can be threatening as it replaces the traditional understanding. Geach (1977, 49) writes that some people have seen this replacement occurring and "desperately look forward to a time when natural science will have progressed so far that we shall not need, in serious thinking, to talk of people's words, opinions, plans and intentions, but only of physical and physiological states and events."

This way of thinking warns against Adler's thought. However, what is needed is a common understanding. Both Geach and Adler in their respective schools of thought understand hope as eschatologically determined. Both see life as striving for a better future. Both understand the notion of the future to be realized in some manner in the present. As we understand Adler and Geach they could assent to the following: "There is a consensus that God is a work in time, bearing with his world, and going before it, making present life intelligible, and filling with hope our present work, suffering, and dying through the future which he holds before us" (Cousins 1972, 146).

The point of clarification that needs to be made is that for Adler, God is understood as the goal represented by community feeling.

Eschatological understanding is at the basis of hope. Hope is exercised in the light of its future goal. In Adlerian psychology the promise of the future inspires individuals in the present and orientates them to community feeling. Similarly, Moltmann's (1967) existential theology of hope does not attempt to construct an ideal picture of future events or conditions. Rather, his theology of hope is an evoked relationship that leads individuals to understand the existing situation and motivates them to effect some sort of transformation in their religious lives. From an Adlerian perspective hope leads individuals to clarify their notion of community feeling. Adler understood the virtue of hope as something found in the notion of human progress. However, in the minds of certain theologians, Adler is mistaken in restricting hope, the movement to community feeling, to the context of progress as he does. Adler (1964, 25) says:

> But social interest is continually pressing and growing. For this reason, no matter how dark the times may be, in the long-range view there is the assurance of the higher development of the individual and the group. Social interest is continually growing; human progress is a function of the higher development of social interest; therefore, human progress will be inevitable as long as mankind exists.

Many theologians understand hope in relation to God who remains outside the influence of progress. However, progress is, in fact, understood as the rationalization and secularization of Christian hope. Brunner (1956, 43) writes: "The idea of progress, we have said, is not a Christian idea. No New Testament writer, no medieval writer, no writer of the Reformation had any idea of progress." James (1909) understands progress as a 20th century phenomenon. Something innate in the individual prompts striving for the future, for the good of the individual, and the community.

Brunner (1956, 52) notes that "the Christian faith does not hope for union; it hopes for communion." This understanding is echoed by Charles Davis. Hope is not something we lack now, waiting for a future realization, but rather hope has its concrete effects in the present living moment. Davis devotes an entire chapter in his book to the subject of the Church and Hope. His understanding of Christian hope realized is that one attains Christian communion in life now. Like Christ, we prevail over every contrary force, including death. Davis (1967, 99) writes:

> Christian hope is not the expectation of a reward after a life essentially
> different from what is to come. It is a trusting assurance that the life in Christ
> we now enjoy will prevail over every contrary force, including death itself.
> We have already been liberated, and our hope is the confidence that the new
> life we have been given is indeed eternal and will endure despite all
> afflictions and even beyond death.

From an Adlerian perspective this trusting assurance leads us to seek a
greater participation in community feeling as it is recognized to be a form
of hope fulfilled. Theologically, our hope is rewarded. Brink suggests that
Adler linked hope and community feeling so closely that, "According to
Adler, once the faith in the future is gone, it becomes very difficult to
maintain social interest and to obtain successful compensation" (Brink
1977, 147). What we hope for is in the process of being realized in the
present moment. Those who live in hope, encourage each other, strengthen
each other and affirm each other in life against hardships and seeming
meaninglessness. But the individual and the community live in the
expectation that their hopes will be realized. "Claims of interest in the
well-being of the community, however, have power in the long run only
if their professed accord with the general well-being finds confirmation,"
says Adler (1964, 27).

From an Adlerian perspective, hope leads the individual to seek a
deepening of community feeling through striving for a better future. For
the Christian there is a tension between the present and the future. This
tension is the lived reality where things longed for and hope realized in
experience do not yet coincide. Adler (1943, 275) notes:

> It is not a question of any present-day community or society, or of political
> or religious forms. On the contrary, the goal that is best suited for perfection
> must be a goal that stands for an ideal society amongst all mankind, the
> ultimate fulfilment of evolution.

This accords with St. Paul's teaching in Romans 8:24ff. Hope is future
directed and its object is not yet accomplished. Otherwise, there would be
no point in hoping. "For who hopes for what he sees? But if we hope for
what we do not see, we wait for it with patience", as the Apostle Paul
expressed it (Romans 8:24).

It is incumbent on the Christian to live "as if" the future is realized in
the present. The notion of "as if" is significant to the understanding of
Individual Psychology. Adler suggests exactly the same notion by his use

of a psychological fiction. The fiction becomes a guiding principle for the individual. A guiding fiction is Adler's way of showing how individuals comprehend their own striving for the future. For Adler, the guiding fiction that the individual constructs, does not necessarily require an objective referent. Further, Brink says: "In order for the guiding fiction to be effective within its role, it is not necessary that its truth claims be valid" (Brink 1977, 146). For the Christian, the role of the guiding fiction is replaced by a belief in God.

Hope establishes a healthy lifestyle. Slavik & Croake (2001, 29) discuss this as an optimistic attitude that "entails a positive outlook on the world, others and ourselves." What the biblical miracles record about change in the individual may be recounted in Adlerian terms. At least this is Brink's notion. By accepting a new guiding fiction, these individuals are released from neurotic life-styles that had manifested themselves in terms of physical maladies (Brink 1977, 148). Adler develops the notion that individuals base their movement on a fictional psychological order of their own construction. For this they must use the power innate in themselves as members of the community. Having established this fictional base the individuals will then act, "*as if* this world were real, true and good for all time" (Becker 1962, 48).

There is an element of risk in life which the individual cannot side step. Life is not certain. Hope, psychologically speaking, offers no philosophical certainty but offers venture.   Noting Anselm's understanding, Thornton (1963, 159) says of faith's dynamic that "it is...a gift to be *used* not *held*" [Thornton's italics]. One who lives in hope confidently lives as if living in knowledge and is thus not subject to the criticism of credulity. It is not unreasonable to see that hope provides a type of assurance similar to a pastoral theology. As Muyskens (1979, 140) observed:

> But if, on the other hand, a Christian theology functions to provide a sense of the direction of life, of its meaning and purpose (not a privileged solace or special knowledge of any sort) then, (I believe) a theology of hope will prove adequate for Christian needs.

The purpose of cognitive therapy is to move to an adequate understanding of the lifestyle of individuals so that the virtue of hope may be fully lived out. Adlerian cognitive therapy sees the goal of human development orientated to the future. With such an attitude an individual can be understood as a creature of hope. Adler conceives the dynamic of hope arising out of the new evolved human condition. Adler's understanding of hope differs in description from a classical theology of hope when it comes to expression but does not differ in intent. Adler (Ansbacker & Ansbacker 1956, 461) says:

> It has taken an unthinkably long time and it has required a large number of tentative attempts for us to recognize a satisfactory image, to experience the revelation of a supreme being who would lead one to the hope and belief of security for the species and for the individual.

He understands that the notion of community feeling is not made concrete in this life but is rather a goal to strive towards. Conceived in its final form this goal of community, posited by humanity at large, inspires hope and those who direct their behaviour to attaining this goal are healthy. From Adler's perspective, the individual living and acting in despair, a lack of hope, displays unhealthy neurotic behaviour. Hope gives meaning and purpose to life that prevents an unhealthy attitude from dominating the individual. The healthy individual finds hope uplifting and motivating as far as the demands of action and work are concerned. The neurotic becomes hypnotized by a simulated life-plan. Two authors, Brink (1977) and Mansager (1987), accept Adler's Individual Psychology as healthful.

Extreme displays of interest in social conditions, self-centeredness and isolation would all be earmarks of the despairing or neurotic person. The normal, non-clinical interpretation of life can be experienced as preparing the individual and the community for future development. In this way Adler's own understanding parallels very closely the Christian virtue of hope as movement towards unrealized expectation. Adler (1943, 285) writes:

> This social feeling exists within us and endeavours to carry out its purpose; it does not seem strong enough to hold its own against all opposing forces. The justified expectation persists that in a far-off age, if mankind is given enough time, the power of social feeling will triumph over all that opposes it.

Having discussed faith and hope as virtues in the context of Adlerian psychology it remains to treat the virtue of charity.

Charity

For Adler there is no notion of self-sacrifice or deficiency attached to charity. O'Connell (2001) expresses a notion of charity that fits well with Adler's understanding. He writes:

Compassion Fatigue is one of my most hated mechanical concepts. It came into vogue in the 80's as a weakego movement designed to make avoidance into an honourable virtuous sacrifice. In truth, no one with true compassion ('social interest', community feelings, universal belonging) ever wears out from using it.

Compassion fatigue does not arise in the proper development of one's abilities for the good of self and the good of others. Brunner (1956, 63/64) tells us that agape (charity) is not grounded in any value, the loveableness of the beloved, or completion of the ego, but it is unmotivated love. That is, charity is not a seeking to act for requited love, but charity is an evoked response (attitude) because one has been loved. Or, from a religious perspective, do for others what God has done for you. Expressed in Adlerian terms, charity means the striving to realize the notion of community feeling. A refusal to show interest in community feeling would not only be uncharitable, according to Adler's cognitive therapy, but neurotic as well. Adler (1943, 283) tells us:

When we speak of virtue we mean that a person plays his part; when we speak of vice we mean that he interferes with co-operation. I can, moreover, point out that all that constitutes a failure is so because it obstructs social feeling, whether children, neurotics, criminals, or suicides are in question.

A concept that Adler struggled with, and in fact came to reject, is that charity is not an extension to others of one's natural self-concern, 'do unto others as you would have them do unto you.' Of the concept of charity found in St. John's gospel, Moffat (1929, 126) writes a paragraph with which Adler would have little quarrel.

What he [John] generally means by the term is not a definite relation towards men and women so much as the sublimated sense of being part of the human whole; it denotes for him man's general duty as a member of the race, an emotion and an idea due to the common humanity of man, as though to be humane and kind was the duty of a human creature as such.

The gospel's intent here is not simply to correct the disciple and encourage abandonment of evil ways and to avoid self-harm and harm to others. Rather, the intent is to increase the health and well-being of the individual. The individual must adapt behaviour to the good of the community. What is healthy for the individual is healthy for the community. The intention in acting charitably is to solve the broad problems of living in community. The paradox is that in solving the broad problems of others we often solve particular problems as well. This striving for the well-being of others is innate in the human character. As Adler (1943, 37) notes:

> Surely the commands, 'thou shalt not kill' and 'Love thy neighbour', can hardly ever disappear from knowledge and feeling as the supreme court of appeal. These and other norms of human social life, which are undoubtedly the products of evolution and are as native to humanity as breathing and the upright gait, can be embodied in the conception of an ideal human community, regarded here as the impulse and the goal of evolution.

Community feeling is meant to bring individuals together for the good of all concerned, Adler often reminds us. The theologian, Charles Davis, is also concerned with a healthy human community. A healthy community is a liberating community and has responded to experiences within the Roman Catholic Communion which were less than healthy. Davis comes to the same conclusion as Adler in positing that human social life ought to be organized to promote unity and fellowship.

Adler (1954) insists that community feeling needs to be developed from birth and he presents this perspective in his earliest writings. Similarly, the Christian insists that charity be exercised from birth. D.L. Weatherhead (1952, 453) understood what Adler was attempting to articulate through his Individual Psychology.

> We defined health, earlier in this book, as the harmonious relationship between every part of the self and Environment. Granted that man is a body, mind and spirit, his complete health necessitates a harmonious relationship between his spirit and its environment which we call God.

Significantly, Weatherhead equates the environment with God. In Adlerian terms this environment occasions the dynamic relationship of community feeling or *Gemeinschaftsgefühl*.

To avoid a pantheistic and thus a mistaken view from the Christian perspective any inquiry must consider the virtues of faith, hope and charity primarily in theological terms, not psychological terms.

Bibliography

Adler, A. 1927. *Understanding human nature*. New York: Greenberg.

—, 1930. Individual Psychology. In *Psychologies of 1930 - The international university series in psychology*, edited by C. Murchison, 395-405. Worcester, Mass: Clark University Press.

—, 1931. *What life should mean to you*. New York: Blue Ribbon Books.

—, 1943. *Social interest: A challenge to mankind*. London: Faber & Faber.

—, 1950. *What life should mean to you*. Boston: Little: Brown.

—, 1954. *Understanding human nature*. New York: Fawcett.

—, 1964. *Superiority and social interest - A collection of later writings*. Evanston: Northwestern University Press.

—, 1964a *The practice and theory of individual psychology*. London: Routledge & Kegan Paul.

Ansbacher, H.L. and R. R. Ansbacher, R.R. 1956. *The individual psychology of Alfred Adler: A systematic presentation in selections from his writings*. New York: Basic Books.

Becker, E. 1962. *The birth and death of meaning*. New York: Free Press of Glencoe.

Beecher, W. and M. Beecher. 1973. Memorial to Alfred Adler. In *Alfred Adler: His influence on psychology today*, edited by H. H. Mosak, 1-5. Park Ridge, NJ: Noyes Press.

Bieliauskas, V. J. 1973. Motivation and the Will. In *Alfred Adler: His influence on psychology today*, edited by H. H. Mosak, 6-18. Park Ridge, NJ: Noyes Press.

Brink, T.L. 1977. Adlerian theory and pastoral counseling. *Journal of Psychology and Theology* 5:(2) 134-49.

Brunner, E. 1956. *Faith, hope and love*. Philadelphia: Westminster Press.

Carver, C. S. and M. F. Scheier. 1996. *Perspectives on personality* (3rd Ed.). Toronto: Allyn and Bacon.

Clinebell, H. 1979. *Growth counseling: Hope-centered methods of actualizing human wholeness*. Abingdon: Nashville.

Cousins, E. H. 1972. *Hope and the future of man*. Philadelphia: Fortress Press.

Davis, C. 1967. *A question of conscience*. London: Hodder & Stoughton.

Dewart, L. 1966. *The future of belief*. New York: Herder & Herder.

Dreikurs, R. 1973. The Private Logic. In *Alfred Adler: His influence on psychology today,* edited by H. H. Mosak, 19-32. Park Ridge, NJ: Noyes Press.

Fancher, R. E. 1996. *Pioneers of psychology* (3rd Ed.). New York: W. W. Norton & Company.

Ferguson-Dreikurs, E. 1995. *Adlerian theory: An introduction.* Chicago: Adler School of Professional Psychology.

Flannery, A. P. 1966. *Vatican Council II: Constitutions, decrees and declarations* (Revised Edition). Costello Publishing: New York.

—, 1975. *Vatican Council II: The conciliar and post conciliar documents.* Grand Rapids: Eerdmans.

Forsyth, J. 1997. *Faith and human transformation: A dialogue between psychology and theology.* Lanham: University Press of America.

Funk and Wagnalls Canadian College Dictionary. 1989. *s.v.* reaction and response. Fitzhenry & Whiteside: Toronto.

Gaybba, B. 1988. *Aspects of the mediaeval history of theology: 12th to 14th centuries.* Pretoria: University of South Africa Press.

Geach, P. 1977. *The virtues.* Cambridge: Cambridge University Press, 1977

Graef, H. 1959. *Modern gloom and Christian hope.* Henry Regnery: Chicago.

Grey, L. 1998. *Alfred Adler, The forgotten prophet: A vision for the 21st century.* West Port: Praeger.

Henry, J. 2001. On religious experience. *Explorations: Journal for Adventurous Thought* 19 (4).

Hoffman, E. 1994. *The drive for self: Alfred Adler and the founding of Individual Psychology.* New York: Addison Wesley.

Hughson, S.C. 1950. *With Christ in God.* London: SPCK.

James, W. 1908. *The varieties of religious experience.* London: Longmans, Green.

Kobler, J. F. 2000. Vatican II's pastoral theology needs philosophy. *The Modern Schoolman* LXXVIII: 89-95.

Krausz, E. O. 1973. Neurotic Versus Normal Reaction Categories. In *Alfred Adler: His influence on psychology today,* edited by H. H. Mosak, 53-7. Park Ridge, NJ: Noyes Press.

Mairet, P. 1930. Introduction. In *The science of living.* London: George Allen & Unwin.

Mansager, E. 1987. One framing of the issue: Adlerian psychology within pastoral counseling. *Individual Psychology: The Journal of Adlerian Theory, Research & Practice* 43 (4): 451-460.

McBrien, R. 1987. *Ministry.* San Francisco: Harper & Row.

McDougall, W. 1930. The Hormic Psychology. In *Psychologies of 1930,* edited by C. Murchison, 3-36. Worcester, Mass: Clark University Press.

Moffatt, J. 1929. *Love in the New Testament.* London: Hodder & Stoughton.

Moltmann, J. 1967. *Theology of hope.* London: SCM Press.

Mosak, H. H. 1973. The Controller: A Social Interpretation of the Anal Character. In *Alfred Adler: His influence on psychology today*, edited by H. H. Mosak, 43-52. Park Ridge, NJ: Noyes Press.

Müller, A. 1992. *You shall be a blessing: Main traits of a religious humanism.* San Francisco: Alfred Adler Institute of San Francisco.

Murry, J. M. 1929. *God: Being an introduction to the science of metabiology.* Cape: London.

Muyskens, J. 1979. *The sufficiency of hope.* Philadelphia: Temple University Press.

O'Connell, W. 2001. Documented correspondence with Allan Savage.

O'Murchu, D. 2000. *Religion in exile: A spiritual homecoming.* New York: Crossroad.

Rom, P. 1973. Distance: Antecedent of alienation. In *Alfred Adler: His influence on psychology today,* edited by H. H. Mosak, 33-42. Park Ridge, NJ: Noyes Press.

Slavik, S. and J. Croake. 1999. *Gemeinschaftsgefühl:* What it isn't and what it is. In *Readings in the Theory and Practice of Adlerian Psychology Selected from the Canadian Journal of Adlerian Psychology.* Victoria, B.C.: Adlerian Psychology Association of British Columbia.

—, 2001. Optimism. *The Canadian Journal of Adlerian Psychology* 31(2): 26-34.

Slavik, S. 2000. The subject matter of Individual Psychology. *The Canadian Journal of Adlerian Psychology* 30(2): 34-44.

Smith, W.C. 1982. *Religious diversity.* New York: Crossroad.

Speber, M. 1974. *Masks of loneliness: Alfred Adler in perspective.* New York: Macmillan.

Stein, H. 2003. A psychology for democracy. *Year Book 2003.* London: Adlerian Society (of the united Kingdom) and the Institute for Individual Psychology.

Summa Theologica. 1948 Fathers of the English Dominican Province (American Edition). New York: Benziger.

Tanquery, A. 1930. *The spiritual life.* New York: Desclee.

Tennant, F.R. 1943. *The nature of belief.* London: The Centenary Press.

Thornton, M.1959. *Christian proficiency.* New York: Morehouse-Gorham.

—, 1963. *English spirituality: An outline of ascetical theology according to the English pastoral tradition.* London: SPCK.

—, 1974. *My God: A reappraisal of normal religious experience.* London: Hodder Stoughton.

Vaihinger, H. 1952. *The philosophy of 'as if': A system of theoretical, practical and religious fictions of mankind.* London: Routledge & Kegan Paul.

Vande Kemp, H. 1985. Psychotherapy as a Religious Process: A Historical Heritage. In *Psychotherapy and the religiously committed patient,* edited by E. M. Stern, 135-146. New York: Haworth.

Weatherhead, L. 1952. *Psychology, religion and healing.* London: Hodder & Stoughton.

CHAPTER 6

EXERCISE IN CRITICAL COLLABORATION BETWEEN MANSAGER AND SAVAGE

Adlerian Psychology and Spirituality in Critical Collaboration

Erik Mansager

Only a few years ago in the United States (and perhaps still here in the European nations), a discussion of a religious topic would take place only after extracting promises that the participants were assured of their anonymity - promised that they would not be named. Living in close quarters with one another as we at ICASSI, none of us are able to remain anonymous. Still, there remains the possibility of great animosity:

- Given the increase of fundamentalism in religions around the world *verses* the effervescence of New Age thought;

- Given the inward assurance of many listening today that this topic could only be addressed by "a truly spiritual person" *verses* the suspicion by all good Individual Psychologists that a person presenting such a topic must surely think of himself as spiritual - both questionable assumptions in this case;

● Given those in the audience who hope for a definitive affirmation of supernatural dimensions at a psychological institute *verses* those in the audience who anticipate a definitive repudiation of supernatural concepts - especially among post-modern Adlerians.

So, in the face of such potential animosity, I ask first not for anonymity but for a degree of non-animosity - for openness to consider the ideas about to be presented.

Holistically-Considered Spirituality

In a single presentation, everything on the topic of spirituality cannot be said. And so I ask a second favour that - while being open to what is offered - the reader forgive what is not said. Holistically speaking, since all the following concepts are actively interconnected, I run the risk of presenting holistic concepts as being disconnected from the whole, or even as if they are discrete entities in themselves. By holistic I mean that the complexity of life is considered free of dualistic, either-or thinking. It describes reality as a process that continually organizes into greater wholes. In regard to human development, it is the dynamic social interconnection of the person that goes beyond the individual. When the whole human person is functioning co-operatively towards the betterment of the whole community, it is then that his or her interests are most likely to be served. Under such circumstances Individual Psychologists speak of wellness.

In considering spirituality holistically, there are a number of interconnected questions to be considered: Who is spiritual? When or where (i.e., under what circumstances) is that person considered spiritual? Why are people spiritual? What constitutes spirituality? How does one express one's spirituality? How does one study spirituality anyway? This article addresses only the more public, communal "what" and "how" questions. Regarding the "what" of spirituality, an initial definition is offered so that the question of "how" to study the topic can be offered to Individual Psychologists. I then return to the "what" with a more detailed, hopefully more useful definition. It is then from this broadened perspective, that a critical collaboration between Individual Psychology and religion becomes possible.

What Is Spirituality?

The context of spirituality for Individual Psychologists falls in the human circumstance Adler described as movement from a felt minus to a fictional [as well as felt] plus (Ansbacher & Ansbacher, 1964). This is the very rhythm of life: hunger - satiation; thirst - quenching; nervousness - relaxation. But when this same rhythm is directed by a person to provide ultimate answers – "Who am I?", "Why am I here?", "What is the meaning of life?" - then such striving is understood as one's "religious sentiment" (Allport 1965/1960, 56).

This sentiment includes both content and process dimensions. The content dimension includes the many communal aspects of dogmas and public rituals as well as personal beliefs and personal rituals, places of worship, sacred clothing, and other tangible matters. In this article such content matters are considered one's "religiosity" (Ingersoll 1994).

The process dimension includes the more personally unique movement of the individual from a felt minus individually perceived plus situation. It involves the personal interpretation of more public religion - or one's non-religious stance. In this article, such matters are considered the stuff of "spirituality" (Hinterkopf, 1994).

How Can Spirituality Be Studied?

Given this initial conceptualization of what spirituality is, a second question can address specifically "how" Individual Psychologists might study the phenomenon in order to better understand it. Among the approaches to studying spirituality from the perspective of psychology, two possibilities deserve special attention: integration of the two and their critical collaboration.

Integration has been the more common approach in Adlerian literature to date. It is, in fact, the method recommended by historian of psychology Hendrika Vande Kemp (2000) to Adlerians interested in studying religion. Historically considered, Fritz Künkel (1938), Rudolf Allers (1939), and Alexander Müller (1954/1992), all took this approach. These authors assented to certain religious beliefs and seemed to apply Individual Psychology in such a way that they adjusted the psychological anthropology to fit their particular religion. It, in effect, offers an integrated anthropology, determined by the religious starting point.

Arguably, this is demonstrated more recently in the works of Erik Blumenthal (1987), Vladimir Smekal (1997) and James Sulliman (May/June 2000). However, Adler strongly objected to this approach whether from the Protestant (Künkel) or Catholic (Allers) perspectives (Ansbacher & Ansbacher 1964, 285 fn. & 286 fn.)

Critical collaboration, the approach I advocate, is one that has yet to be broadly applied. Both aspects of the term, critique and collaboration, pertain to religion as well as psychology.

From the religious perspective:

- Collaboration entails the believer using psychology to understand the meaning of interpersonal and intrapersonal wellness for the individual.

- Criticism involves standing against psychological pronouncements that intend to explain ultimate reality, truth, being, and the like. The realm of ultimate concern properly belongs to religion (Küng 1994).

Also from the psychological perspective:

- Collaboration entails respectful attempts at understanding human longing after an ultimate source of meaning (Emmons 1999) as well as acceptance that being fully human includes ultimate concerns which are beyond psychological explanation.

- Criticism involves an ongoing critique of religious and spiritual expressions that hinder fully human development - interpersonal and intrapersonal wellness.

So, critical collaboration is a reciprocal enterprise within which psychology acknowledges religious-spiritual responses as important human experience while providing a responsible, ongoing critique of the humaneness of such responses. At the same time religion and spirituality as practised by the individual and the community, represent human beings consciously engaged in their ultimate concerns.

Individual Psychology, as a critical collaborator represents a valid, intellectual setting for understanding religiously and spiritually oriented persons.

While both integration and critical collaboration are helpful in understanding spirituality, critical collaboration has been largely missing from the Individual psychology literature. In the greater body of religious studies, collaboration is frequently seen among psychologists (Hood, Spilka, Hunsberger & Gorsuch 1996, Pargament 1997), sociologists (Argyle & Beit-Hallahmi 1975, Stark 1967), pathologists (Shafranske 1996, Solignac 1982), and philosophers (Brody 1974, Abernethy & Langford 1968). But for fear of an integrationist agenda, there is little collaboration with theologians and pastors (Ellis 2000, Strunk 1970). However, within the last dozen years or so, a new type of critical theologian has developed within the study of spirituality, considered as an academic discipline (Schneiders 1998).

Much as academic psychology studies the psychology active within individuals and groups - personality, motivation, character traits, and the like - so, too, does spirituality as an academic discipline study the spirituality within individuals and groups - their personally transformative experiences. Prominent among this movement is the call for psychology to collaborate by focussing on the human person (Schneiders 1998). Since it is the person who is the subject of the transformational experience, it is appropriate to appeal to the study of the individual via psychological enquiry. This focus calls for psychology to collaborate as psychology and not by recreating a religious anthropology - thereby distorting the psychology on which the scholar has drawn. From this perspective, Sandra Schneiders (1986, 266) has suggested a definition of spirituality that is widely acknowledged as a consensus among diverse fields. Spirituality, according to Schneiders' definition, is "the experience of consciously striving to integrate one's life in terms not of isolation and self-absorption, but of self-transcendence toward the ultimate value one perceives."

Critiquing Spiritual Wellness

Schneiders (1998) exhibits great sensitivity to a wide interdisciplinary approach. Thus, exploration of her definition (Schneiders 1986) from the perspective of Individual Psychology promises the possibility of arriving at an understanding of personal transformational experience - spirituality - that does not require distorting Individual Psychology with religious concepts in order to do so.

Striving

Striving is not just periodic conscious activity aimed towards a current, short-term goal. Rather, striving is the very activity of life. Life is movement towards an end state - not only that which we know, but also that towards which we can only hope and seek "as if" it exists. Not only the minus of desire and the plus of satisfaction and completion; but also that striving towards which a given individual lives as his or her ultimate concern, final goal, "eternal destiny."

Because of our social embeddedness, such completion seeks connection and belonging within the greater community. It seeks connection to everybody and everything. In this sense the spiritual dimension is not separate from the social dimension. From this perspective, Individual Psychology is prepared to offer criteria for measuring the wellness of the striving dimension of spirituality. One can measure the benefit of an individual's spirituality by considering whether the striving after one's ultimate concern manifests as co-operation on the communally useful, contributing side of life rather than on the self-serving side of life (Mansager 2000).

Integration

Whereas most theories understand integration to be a conscious activity involved in the maturing individual, Individual Psychologists accept that a significant integration is accomplished in each individual from a very early age. Rather than understanding life as a unifying process, Individual Psychologists recognize each individual as already unified. It is recognizing the individuals unifying goal and altering it on a conscious level that is the difficult task of maturing. The principle of holism accounts for an integrated style of living – one's lifestyle. This holistic understanding is a major contribution of Individual Psychology to the understanding of personality and consequently to the understanding of spirituality. The characteristically unified movement of the individual towards his or her goal is recognizable whether a person believes in a god or not.

Conscious holistic thinking comes only with age, however. Children first orient themselves by thinking antithetically - thinking in opposites: up or down; here or there; dark or light. They are introduced to god concepts in a similar fashion (good or bad; all-knowing or ignorant; all-loving or hateful) long before they are able to perform abstract thinking. So their ideas of god are well established before their ability to reformulate an idea dialectically - without believing it actually exists as they initially conceived of it.

Adults continue to use antithetical thinking to orient themselves. However, they too often forget to re-think these constructs more abstractly and confuse early formulations of god as directly correlated to reality. It is an insight of Individual Psychology that strict adherence to such orienting devices represents a lowered measure of relative wellness. The ability to revise one's viewpoint, as more reliable data become available, represents a measure of greater wellness. Such a measure of wellness can be applied whether an individual retains a steadfast adherence to a religious tradition or not since adherence to a core set of beliefs need not be manifested as intolerance (Küng 1990/1991). Still, a criterion for evaluating spiritual integration from the psychological perspective can be made by determining whether one's spiritual path is closed, judgmental, and prejudiced rather than open, tolerant and flexible (Mansager 2000).

Self Transcendence

Thinking of transcendence in terms of a supernatural dimension is undoubtedly still appealing to many. For more and more contemporaries, however, a transcendent "out there" is no longer a viable concept. Adler himself subscribed to a certain metaphysics (as cited in Ansbacher & Ansbacher 1964). He understood that all new thought, ideas and theory come from speculating about the unknown. Nonetheless, he saw all of reality connected in a single universe. While earth-bound humans are connected to the far reaches of the universe, he contended, there is no other realm beside it (Adler 1927/1998, 35). This connection, as all human bonds, is a social one. The self-bounded person is a mistaken understanding of the social human being. People are indivisibly enmeshed in a social world. Transcendence is first and foremost movement away from radical independence and towards a more accurately understood interdependence - to a feeling of oneness with the community, *Gemeinschaftsgefühl*.

So, a criterion for measuring spiritual transcendence is also available. It has to do with one's perception of being connected beyond one's self, being part of and contributing to the greater community. The degree to which the individual's spirituality leads away from isolation and self-absorption and towards the greater community is a measure of that person's relative wellness (Mansager 2000).

Ultimate Value

How the individual defines his or her goal of perfection - usually in a manner in which the person is not fully aware - is the essential aspect of our life style. Individuals live "towards" that which is most valued - both in the short term as well as in the long run. The ultimate goal one posits for oneself "signifies life" (Adler, as cited in Ansbacher & Ansbacher

1964, 277). According to Adler, this is due to the striving that always flows from insecurity - the constant inferiority feeling of needy humanity. As striving begins, humans aim towards the non-striving - the complete. It was in this way, Adler suggests, that the idea of a monotheistic god eventually dawned on humanity after eons of trial and error: the concept that promises security for the individual and for the group.

The activity of critical collaboration can be seen clearly in this instance. While a person's idea of ultimate value - be it God, is, nevertheless at least that - an idea. And this cognitive aspect is the avenue that allows psychology to critique such conceptualization as humane or not. However, should an Individual Psychologist pronounce that the idea is real or not - he or she would be due the criticism of the religious counterpart. It is not the question of real or not real, true or false, that is the concern of Individual Psychology. It is rather how this ultimate value affirms or contradicts one's spiritual movement - the striving, integration, and self-transcendence.

One's ultimate value, ultimate concern, itself becomes a meta-criterion for measuring personal wellness - of evaluating the health of one's spirituality. To the degree that one's highest value encourages useful striving (vs. useless), to the degree that it encourages integrating open-mindedness (vs. antithetical judgments), to the degree that it encourages self-transcendence towards greater community interest (vs. self-boundedness for personal interests) - to that degree one's highest value is a valid criterion for measuring one's wellness (Mansager 2000).

Conclusion

Hopefully, the opportunity that lies ahead for Individual Psychologists is clearer now than before. I have intended to show that by collaboratively critiquing a broadly accepted definition of spirituality from the perspective of Individual Psychology, it is possible to arrive at a tentative understanding of "what" spirituality is without distorting Adler's theory. Although time does not allow further exploration of "how" spiritual wellness might be understood by the Individual Psychologist, practical application of Adlerian techniques to the individual's transformative experiences awaits further attention.

REFERENCES

Abernethy, G. L. and T. A. Langford. 1968. *Philosophy of religion: A book of readings* (2nd ed.). New York: Macmillan.

Adler, A. 1927/1998. *Understanding human nature.* Center City, MN: Hazelden.

Allers, R. 1939. *The psychology of character.* New York: Macmillan.

Allport, G. W. 1951/1960. *The individual and his religion.* New York: Macmillan.

Ansbacher, H. L. and R. R. Ansbacher. 1964. *Superiority and social interest.* New York: Norton.

Argyle, M. and B. Beit-Hallahmi. 1975. *The social psychology of religion.* Boston: Routledge & Kegan Paul.

Blumenthal, E. 1987. *The meaning of life.* Course conducted within the Adlerian Summer Institute, ICASSI, Noordwijkerhout, The Netherlands.

Brody, B. A. 1974. *Readings in the philosophy of religion: An analytic approach.* Englewood Cliffs, NJ: Prentice-Hall.

Ellis, A. 2000. Can rational emotive behavior therapy be effectively used with people who have devout beliefs in God and religion? *Professional Psychology* 31: 29-33.

Emmons, R. A. 1999. *The psychology of ultimate concerns.* New York: Guilford.

Hinterkopf, E. 1994. Integrating spiritual experiences in counseling. *Counseling and Values* 38: 165-75

Hood, R. W., B. Spilka, B. Hunsberger and R. Gorsuch. 1996. *The psychology of religion.* New York: Guilford.

Ingersoll, R. E. 1994. Spirituality, religion, and counseling. *Counseling and Values* 38: 98-111.

Küng, H. 1990/1991. *Global responsibility. In Search of a New World Ethic.* London: SCM Press.

—, 1994. Vorword [Foreword]. In *Relgion als chance oder risiko. Entwicklungsfordernde und entwicklungshemmende aspekte religioser erziehung,* edited by G. Klosinski, 9-12. Bern: Hans Huber.

Künkel, F. 1938. *Character, growth, education.* Philadelphia: Lippincott.

Mansager, E. 2000. Individual psychology and the study of spirituality. *Journal of Individual Psychology* 56(3): 371-88.

Müller, A. 1954/1992. *You shall be a blessing.* San Francisco: Alfred Adler Institute of San Francisco.

Pargament, K. I. 1997. *The psychology of religion and coping. Theory, research, practice.* New York: Guilford.

Schneiders, S. M. 1986. Theology and spirituality: Strangers rivals or partners? *Horizons* 13: 253-74.

—, 1998. The study of Christian spirituality: Contours and dynamics of a discipline. *Christian Spirituality Bulletin* 6 (1): 3-12.

Shafranske, E. P. 1996. *Religion and the clinical practice of psychology.* Washington, D.C.: American Psychological Association.

Smekal, V. 1997. *The future of Individual Psychology.* Unpublished lecture within Adlerian Summer Institute, ICASSI, conducted at Schladming, Austria.

Solignac, P. 1982. *The Christian neurosis.* New York: Crossroad.

Stark, W. 1967. *The sociology of religion* (Vol. 2). London: Routledge & Kegan Paul.

Strunk, O. 1970. Humanistic Religious Psychology: A New Chapter in the Psychology of Religion. *Journal of Pastoral Care* 24 (2): 90-7.

Sulliman, J. R. 2000 President's letter. *The NASAP Newsletter* 33 (3): 2-6.

Vande Kemp, H. 2000. Wholeness, holiness, and the care of souls: The Adler-Jahn debate in historical perspective. *Journal of Individual Psychology* 56 (3): 242-56.

§   §   §

Remarks Concerning Erik Mansager's Article:
Adlerian Psychology and Spirituality in Critical Collaboration

Allan Savage

I thank Dr. Mansager for the opportunity to comment on his article and I appreciate the decision by the Adlerian Year Book editors to print my remarks. My response takes the form of a Christian theological critique that I trust does not lessen its value for Adlerian psychologists. Humans need to know both intellectually (spiritually) and practically (religiously). When we know who we are intellectually, we express it practically, and when we know who we are spiritually, we express it religiously. In short, religion is the practical aspect of spiritual knowledge. Spirituality and Adlerian psychology in critical collaboration hint at more than just Mansager's suggestion that a "practical application of Adlerian techniques to the individual's transformative experiences" can open the door to a

Christian anthropology and enlighten the individual beyond mere intellectual knowledge. I agree, whole-heartedly, that spirituality, (intellectually or theologically understood), may be undertaken collaboratively with Adlerian psychology without distorting Adler's theories. However, while not differing in essentials, I would interpret a few points raised in Dr. Mansager's present article differently with respect to critical collaboration between Adlerian psychology and spirituality.

Firstly, I suggest that rather than understanding spirituality as an attribute of a person, an attribute one may or may not possess, spirituality is better understood as being constitutive of a person. As constitutive of a person, spirituality is one abiding aspect of the individual's identity. One's physical body, also constitutive of a person, is the other abiding aspect of the individual's identity. Loss of a constitutive element means the loss of personal identity. The psychology of a person may change over time without any loss of personal identity. The psychology of the child is not the psychology of the adult. In some sense, the same individual's personal identity remains intact over time. In this understanding, spirituality does not change over time but develops and matures as the individual person strives to meet desired goals. The answer to Dr. Mansager's question, (although not addressed in his article), "Who is spiritual?" is that all humans are spiritual by constitution.

Secondly, I agree that the notion of "integration" ought to be abandoned in favour of the notion of "critical collaboration". In this specific case, however, rather than cite Küng to support this view, I would suggest the thinking of George Tyrrell (1907). Tyrrell's theological critique of the role of psychology in promoting the wellness of the person almost parallels Adler's psychological thought. This should not be surprising given the fact that Adler (1870-1937) and Tyrrell (1861-1907) are somewhat contemporaries in discussing psychological issues in the context of turn-of-the-century ideas. Like Adler, Tyrrell does support Mansager's point which is that collaboration between psychology and spirituality is possible without "... recreating a religious anthropology - thereby distorting the psychology on which the scholar has drawn."

Thirdly, and this is a most significant point in my estimation, is that transcendence does not mean supernatural as Mansager clearly notes. George Tyrrell (1907, 167-171) coined the term "over-natural," to describe the spiritual notions which are entirely within the natural order and which arise out of an intellectual need on the part of individuals. This form of spirituality is what the ancients knew as a philosophical metaphysics. Humans, by nature, participate in the world and an "over world" as they form community or *Gemeinschaftsgefühl*. Movement of an individual towards his or her goal does not depend on whether one believes in God or not, as Mansager has observed. A psychological, an intellectual or a legal fiction, or a philosophical metaphysics are all sufficient in moving the individual from a felt minus to a felt plus both intellectually and practically. Moving from a felt minus to a felt plus through a given spiritual experience (not "over world") shifts us from an intellectual understanding to a religious understanding.

A religious movement from a felt minus to a felt plus can be articulated by a Christian anthropology. Rather than remain confined to relationships in this world, intellectual or otherwise, collaboration between Adlerian psychology and spirituality has the potential to reveal an entirely new understanding of personal transcendence. Adlerian psychology in collaboration with Christian spirituality (anthropology) has the potential to open a truly transcendental cognitive experience (a personal transformational experience) of well-being for the individual and the community. I accept Mansager's notion that "Individual Psychology, as a critical collaborator, represents a valid, intellectual setting for understanding religiously and spiritually oriented persons", not through the "what" of spirituality but as "who" is striving towards a future goal. To my mind, this is in keeping with Adler's (1931, 12) remark on the relationship between Individual Psychology and religion: "We approach the problem from a different angle, but the goal is the same - to increase interest in others."

Adler, A. 1931. *What life should mean to you.* New York: Blue Ribbon Books.
Tyrrell, G. 1907. *Through Scylla and Charybdis: The old theology and the new.* London: Longmans, Green.

§   §   §

Reply to Allan Savage's Comments on My Original Article

Erik Mansager

In brief reply, I will comment on Dr. Savage's three salient points. First, I would agree that spirituality is not one among many attributes of the individual, but constitutive of being human. However, I would contend that a holistic understanding cannot dichotomise between one's physical body and one's spirituality as if a person "has" a spirit in some fashion juxtaposed to a body. This is dualism par excellence. A more holistic approach becomes apparent in response to Dr. Savage's second point.

I am very grateful for having Tyrrell's (1907) theological critique brought to my attention and will take seriously the recommendation to familiarize myself with it. Still, it is the Swiss theologian Hans Küng who is representative to me of theology wholly escaping the dualism of scholastic thinking. He is credited with the formulation that the religious dimension is not somehow separate from the person's human dimensions and thereby connected to a supernatural level. Rather, for him spirituality is a holistically conceived aspect of the individual. Küng (1994) comments, "Religious wishes differ from others not through a special psychic quality, but through their 'object'." For him, wishes are only specifically religious wishes if they have to do in any form with that "'religion' of the absolute or infinite" often designated by the term of God and focussed on "a *definitive* fulfilment of meaning in life and death" (paragraph II. 8, emphasis in original, current author's translation).

Lastly, in acknowledging our different understandings of spirituality (supernatural vs. humanistic), the burden of proof falls to the religious believer as to whether a philosophical metaphysics is insufficient for moving the individual from a felt minus to a felt plus intellectually and practically, but not religiously. I believe such proof could only be provided by giving a mutually understandable (non-dualistic) explanation as to what is insufficient in the philosophical approach and would include indicating how a religious approach differs in its fictive quality from one that is philosophical, legal or psychological.

I hope our differences, respectfully stated, show the importance of making room for critical collaboration beside an integrative approach to psychology and spirituality.

References

Küng, H. 1994. *Antwort an Prof. H. Henseler* [Answer to Prof. H. Henseler]. Tübingen: Author.

Tyrrell, G. 1907. *Through Scylla and Charybdis: The old theology and the new.* London: Longmans, Green.

The Spiritual Aspect of Adlerian Psychology and the Theological Virtues

Allan Savage

What First Must Be Said

I write as a theologian who has recently accepted, with appropriate adaptation, the Individual Psychology of Alfred Adler as a basis for counselling offered by pastors who affirm: In the ministry of Jesus is found the source, the inspiration, the ideal for our study [of persons] (Kemp 1947, 6). Although never formally trained in Adlerian psychology, I recognize today that I have employed the common sense approach reflected in Adlerian Psychology in my pastoral counselling over the last twenty years or so. Although I write from within a Roman Catholic context, I write not as a theologian in the service of the church but rather as a theologian probing into a life-style issue. Mine is a critical ecumenical theology defined by Küng (1995, 215) as " at the same time *practical* and *pastoral*, concerned with life, renewal and reform" [author's emphasis]. This manuscript is an attempt at an interdisciplinary understanding. The issue I address is the increasing inability of the scholastic formulation of the theological virtues to be workable in the contemporary Western context. History shows that scholastic dissatisfaction is more a problem of Roman Catholic ministry than Reformed ministry. Reformed thinking met challenges that Roman Catholic thinking did not. "The Protestant Reformation brought about many changes....The Catholic Church continued the confessional as it was;...but Protestantism, in the main, developed a different approach and philosophy toward the needs and problems of the individual" (Kemp 1947, 39). Individual Psychology may be of current use in Roman Catholic thinking.

Expressed in Adlerian terms, the problem is that the scholastic understanding of the theological virtues hinders rather than promotes community feeling. I write to explore rather than to inform and focus on the relationship between Individual Psychology and a contemporary theological issue. In short, I explore the theological virtues of Faith, Hope and Charity from "the spiritual aspect of Adlerian psychology" (Ansbacher 1999, 16). The pastor, (L. *Pascere,* to feed), as counsellor and the counsellor as pastor share to some degree a common life style which seeks to promote community feeling. There may be something of benefit to both the pastor and counsellor in this brief exploration.

Introduction

Alfred Adler, Jewish-born, converted to Protestantism in later life but not out of religious conviction (Hoffman 1994). However, many of his ideas are useful within a Christian spiritual understanding but psychologists are loathe to discuss them (Mosak & Dreikurs 1967). It is known that Adler remained independent and neutral "....as toward the efforts of Catholic or Protestant psychologists to combine [his] views with religious doctrine" (Hoffman 1994, 194). Despite not being a supporter of organized religion, however, Hoffman (ibid.) notes that Adler would himself collaborate with the Lutheran pastor, Ernest Jahn, in a religious work, *Religion and Individual Psychology.*

The question is: can the general role of the pastor and the counsellor be favourably compared? Each seeks to help the individual achieve some degree of harmony in life. Each seeks to promote the welfare of the individual and community. The purpose of spiritual direction or pastoral psychology, as it is known in the Roman Catholic tradition, is the betterment of the individual. In theology and psychology, on an individual and collective basis, the well-being of the person in intended.

Adler's psychology of living is shaped through participating in life and not merely by observing it. Hence, it is an existential psychology. In contrast, Roman Catholic philosophical thought has tended officially to oppose existential psychological thinking (Leo XIII, *Aeterni Patris*). But, Bernard Lonergan (1968) suggests that Catholic theology has to learn to draw on the new sciences of religion, psychology and sociology. Contemporary Christian theological interpretation cannot rely on one philosophical structure but must necessarily participate in other ways of understanding (i.e., psychological). Vatican Council II applied this principle of alternative understanding to itself, the Church, the People of God. "By its nature and mission the Church is universal in that it is not committed to any one culture or any political, economic or social system" (Flannery 1975, 942).

Adler's psychology is multifaceted with humanistic, cognitive, existential, behavioural and psychodynamic aspects. The existential aspect of Adler's psychology provides the pastor with an opportunity to draw upon new ways of thinking. Gladson and Lucas (1989) suggest that since Sigmund Freud and Carl Jung seem overworked with respect to psychology and religious themes, new ground might be explored in the psychologies of Viktor Frankl and Alfred Adler.

Adler's existential psychology is among those interpretive non-scholastic systems that are becoming more suitable for pastors and/or counsellors. Derrik de Kerckhove (1995, 35) suggests that "the secret of inventing and innovating is lifting information from one context and placing it in another." In this exploration, I appropriate psychological information to pastoral interpretation and introduce the spiritual aspect of Adler's Individual Psychology to understanding the theological Virtues.

The Life Style Issue: an Epistemological Dichotomy (a Split Understanding)

In the West, the prevailing philosophical structure for interpreting the theological virtues is scholastic philosophy. From a counselling perspective, the unsatisfactory aspect of this traditional approach is the dichotomy between subject and object, that is, the split between the knower and the known, the one and the many. This dichotomy is the legacy of Cartesian dualism which has its roots in the philosophy of Plato (427-347 BCE). The thinking of René Descartes (1596-1650) led to a popular acceptance of the mind as subject and the body as object. This dichotomy between subject and object does not promote community feeling. In the contemporary Western context, this dichotomy does not help in formulating a cohesive pattern or movement to cope with life's difficulties. Holism, which is the philosophical theory that a living organism has a reality other than and greater than the sum of its constitutive parts, promotes community feeling.

In the context of a self-creative holistic understanding, Smuts (1926, 243) writes of the human will: "our will is individualistic and has to be harmonized and through effort and struggle to be adjusted to higher ethical and spiritual ends and ideals." In order to promote community feeling, I propose an understanding of the theological virtues which presupposes an ontological unity (a holistic understanding of being) and rejects the scholastic dichotomy. Further, in order to promote community feeling, I suggest that Wuellner's dichotomous epistemological, hence unsatisfactory, definitions of faith, hope and charity need to be recast in existential terms. Wuellner (1966, 103) defines the theological virtue of faith as being "the supernatural assent by which the intellect ....clings to revealed truths because of the authority of God revealing;" the theological virtue of hope as "the act of deliberately expecting to attain with divine help a future good related to man's supreme good (1966, 125); and the theological virtue of charity as the habitual love of someone for the sake of God .... because God loves His own goodness which He wills men to share in created likeness of it" (1966, 49). Alternative existential definitions are developed below.

It needs to be recognized that the dichotomous legacy of scholastic philosophy is not false. Rather the pastor and counsellor should recognize that as a genuine promoter of community feeling such philosophy is no longer adequate for Western culture. To promote community feeling, a Platonic epistemological understanding ought to be replaced by an ontological existential understanding which, while distinguishing between subject and object, holds to the unified existence of the individual. Shelley (2000) provides insight here.

A Life Style Perspective: An Ontological Unity (A Holistic Understanding)

Marcel (1965, 38) in his existentialist diary writes that "the growing consciousness of our need for ontology is surely one of the most striking features of present-day thought ..." I suggest our need for an ontological understanding can be somewhat satisfied through Adler's Individual Psychology.

There are methods of interpretation which do not have their roots in scholastic philosophy and are legitimate interpretive tools, such as Indian, East Asian and Native American ways of thinking, These methods of interpretation are psychological methods of existential understanding. During the reformation, existential psychological interpretation and thinking, as an outgrowth of pre-Enlightenment humanism, became friendly towards the Church (Müller 1992).

However, Kemp (1947, 41) notes:

Most of the histories of this period are histories of controversy and most of the preachers referred to are mentioned because of the part they played in some controversy ... but, occasionally, one will catch an incidental reference .... that indicates that men did not lose the pastoral concern for people even in the midst of such periods of debate and conflict.

Such friendliness towards Christian existential thinking was encouraged by Sören Kierkegaard (1813-1855). It is continued in Adlerian thought.

Individual Psychology assists us in moving from *knowing* about faith, hope and charity, an epistemological philosophical concept, to *being* in faith, hope and charity, an existential psychological concept. This existential psychological concept can be developed within the spiritual aspect of Adlerian psychology.

To be or not to be is the more properly holistic approach than to know or not to know, Through a holistic (ontological) lifestyle, self-esteem and a sense of being at home in the world are increased. In his history of pastoral counselling, psychological developments "necessitated a re-thinking and re-evaluating of [a pastor's] historic function of the 'cure of souls' in light of the new insights and discoveries that were being uncovered" (Kemp 1947, 69).

We have, living existentially, the capacity to determine what we will become, that is, to give objective purpose to our striving in life. This objective purpose of social interest or interaction with humans, as Ansbacher (1999) describes it, can achieve greater success when lived in faith, hope and charity. Since we can be other than what we presently are, the future is literally in our hands as we make decisions that shape our environment which in turn shapes us (De Kerckhove, 1995). This understanding is significant for the promotion of social interest in the contemporary world. In Adlerian thought *to be*, or better, *being socially interested*, (a holistic understanding), is the preferred understanding rather than *to know* or *knowing*.

Notions arising out of Adler's Individual Psychology are becoming more acceptable within the contemporary Western context. However, Rahner and Vorgrimler (1973, 324) warn that ontological understanding has its limitations and " makes no claim at all to be the sole and absolute explanation of human life." Yet, Adler's Individual Psychology presents to us a workable holistic notion to the contemporary life-style issue of understanding faith, hope and charity.

Faith: the Community Feeling of Being Faithful Promotes Social Interest

Unlike Wuellner's understanding of faith, whereby the intellect clings to truth, the Adlerian way of understanding faith is that one is faithful in wholesome relationships. Being faithful is a relational concept, not an epistemological concept. Being faithful involves being faithful to others, responding to others, (divinity included), and to oneself. Being faithful is the psychological response process of an individual living in community. Adler (1964, 278) recognises this communal response when he writes of "the possibilities of psychological joining with others." Further, being faithful is a fundamental spiritual attitude which strengthens community. As being faithful leads to an appreciation of other individuals, it also leads to the appreciation of that which is divine in the individual (Slavik, 1994).

In the West, the idea of divinity is incarnated (concretised) in the Christian cultural image of God (Müller 1992). This cultural image of God is presently problematic. Dewart (1989) observes that Western culture is sufficiently empirically minded to find it difficult to affirm that a divine reality really exists but our consciousness allows that perhaps it does. This is a deliberate act of choice and Slavik's (2000, 50) understanding is that Adler developed a notion of consciousness that "is the result of deliberate self-examination through which one brings oneself and one's biases more in accord with common sense and the common good." Notwithstanding this issue, in the Christian tradition, a personal faith relationship is claimed with one Jesus of Nazareth. Jesus' approach to life, and his faithful relationship with others, is a primary example of what Adler intends by social interest.

In probing the issue of being faithful further, the question arises: What is the nature of the divinity with whom we have a wholesome relationship? In Adlerian thought, divinity is not conceived as a pre-existent being (this notion has been inherited from Aristotelian thinking). Rather, divinity is conceived through a process of differentiation of the self from the non-self during the development of human conscious expression. In this process: "There is the individual decision, most often made non-consciously, to believe in God or not" (Mosak & Dreikurs 1967, 17). It seems that Mosak and Dreikurs did not take into account agnostics. Differentiation does not make divinity exist. The idea of divinity arises from participating in a self-conscious life. Our relationship with divinity affectively influences our interest in community feeling and promotes social interest.

In Adlerian thought, divinity does not precede the notion of community feeling. That which is divine, conceived as a being who has loved us first, would be rejected in Individual Psychology. Rather, in Adlerian thinking that which is divine and the notion of community feeling must be understood co-terminally. Ferré (1967) suggests that God is better depicted as a subject disclosed in an existential context of faith rather than depicted as an object of faith. Further, that which is divine and the notion of community feeling *necessarily* relate to each other. Adler's term for this relationship is *Gemeinschaftsgefühl* (Hoffman 1994).

Adlerian psychology is open to assist a pastor/counsellor in relating to others authentically with an improved response to divine presence. In attempting to facilitate this response, pastors/counsellors aim at improving the health and well-being of an individual by working within the life context. Further, (Slavik & Croake 1994) note that *Gemeinschaftsgefühl* is not a measurable concept; it is not based on positivism. Nor is divinity a measurable concept. In Adlerian thinking, being faithful cannot be conceived as possessing an object but rather must be conceived as a relationship between the individual and the other (the divine included). This understanding promotes community feeling. The goal of community feeling, theologically expressed as incarnating the spiritual, discloses one's being faithful not to a reified object but to an attitude in which one relates to another, the divine included, and relates to oneself. In short, the goal of community feeling of being faithful is social interest.

Social interest, or striving to incarnate the spiritual subject, at the present moment, is not sufficiently developed to provide the conditions for a perfect community of faith, that is, a full concretizing (incarnating) of the idea of that which is divine. Rather, we live in hope of establishing a fully developed community of faith. The community of faith, at present, is only partially developed. Being faithful means living in community with a fundamental spiritual attitude that must be content with something less while hoping for something more. Or, in Adlerian terms, one moves from a felt minus to a felt plus.

Hope: the Community Feeling of Being Hopeful Promotes Social Interest

For Wuellner (1966), hope is the act of expecting to attain a future good (goal) whereas an Adlerian view of hope necessarily incorporates the notion of present well-being along with expectation of a future goal. Adler (1964, 275) writes:

> One concretization of the idea of perfection, the highest image of greatness and superiority, which has always been very natural for man's thinking and feeling, is the contemplation of a deity. To strive toward God, to be in him, to follow his call, to be one with Him - from this goal of striving (not a drive), there follow attitude, thinking and feeling.

By striving towards God, Adler means to assign a purposeful, transcendent meaning to life. Hope gives meaning and purpose to human life, but meaning and purpose not understood in Aristotelian terms. Hope prevents an unhealthy attitude from dominating an individual. This meaning and purpose given to human life through hope is revealed through promoting community feeling.

Hope is directed towards a better future. The future orientation of hope is what enjoins the pastor and Adlerian counsellor to promote community feeling. This psychological striving for community feeling is recognized theologically by Christians as living in hope. The promise anticipated in the future inspires us in the present and directs our striving for immediate social interest. Community feeling encourages social interest. Thus, the future is experienced in the present as it were. We live "as if" the future were present. There is no ontological dichotomy in this way of understanding. Striving for social interest in hope, we are led to seek improvements in the present while directing our efforts to the future betterment of the individual and the community. Brink (1977, 147) suggests that Adler linked hope and social interest so closely that: "According to Adler, once the faith in the future is gone, it becomes very difficult to maintain social interest and obtain successful compensation." As community feeling increases (or, for the Christian, as life lived in the spirit increases), so hopefulness increases (Müller 1992).

Those who live in hope, a fundamental spiritual attitude, encourage each other, strengthen each other and affirm each other against hardships and seeming meaninglessness of the present moment. An Adlerian understanding of hope, while directed to the future, encourages us to make improvements in the present, thus promoting social interest. In short, making improvements in the present is the *expression* of social interest.

Being hopeful, existentially speaking, offers no certainty but offers venture. Being hopeful reveals a spiritual meaning and purpose to life that is future directed but enacted in the present. This, is turn, encourages the Christian to practise charity.

Charity: the Community Feeling of Being Charitable Promotes Social Interest

An Adlerian understanding of charity is that of being charitable, not giving charity. That contrasts with Wuellner's (1966) understanding in which we are charitable for the sake of God's goodness shared with us. Or, we are charitable because our view is that God is charitable. In Adlerian thought, charity is not understood as self-sacrifice for others but as a development of our abilities to promote social interest. Being charitable results in a relationship with others and is directed to the good of the individual and the community. Traditionally, in Western theology, the commands to love and not to kill are attributed to a transcendent source. However, Adler (1943, 37) understands them as evolving innately in the human being.

> Surely the commands, "Thou shalt not kill" and "Love thy neighbour", can hardly ever disappear from knowledge and feeling as the supreme court of appeal. These and other norms of human social life, which are undoubtedly the products of evolution are as native to humanity as breathing and the up-right gait, can be embodied in the conception of an ideal human community, regarded here as the impulse and goal of evolution.

A concept with which Adler struggles, and in fact comes to reject, is that being charitable is not a mere extension to others of our natural self-concern. Interestingly, "Do to others as you would have them do to you" (Matthew 7:12) cannot be accepted as an Adlerian formulation since this decision may be restricted to the present moment. The Adlerian formulation of being charitable is more open-ended than that. Being charitable involves our innate community feeling for others, a transcendent notion that deliberately considers the benefit of future generations. Being charitable means living one's life in the promotion of social interest, not simply avoiding harming others. The community feeling of being charitable looks beyond the present moment of the individual life or generation.

Interpreting Adler, Müller (1992, 53) writes: "Life received from no one, also serves no one." This Adlerian formulation of charity is supported by Marcel (1965, 69) who writes: "At the heart of charity is presence in the sense of the absolute gift of one's-self, a gift which implies no impoverishment of the giver."

It is interesting to note that Frost (1996, 114) claims that:

> life is a process which seems to defy entropy, the second law of thermodynamics. It holds that all centres of energy will dissipate in the long run .... [However,] life is a monument of gathering momentum and increasing its centres of energy ongoingly. Vitalists delight in such insights.

The gift of giving ourselves does not deplete us. Rather, it enriches our lives. Being charitable cannot be a selfish act.

Being charitable, of necessity, requires that individuals become involved with their immediate community and the larger community. In acting charitably, individuals promote social interest and enter a new way of living, or better, a new way of being (Müller 1992). Theologically, Moffatt (1929, 109) makes the same observation in a specifically Christian context:

> The hope of the Kingdom was that such inward relationships to God would then become the law of human life; but, while Jesus was no mere futurist, he lived under the apocalyptic hope in such a way as to believe in the urgency of the new law for those who were the nucleus of the new order.

O'Connell (1997, 108) puts the same notion this way: "Sentimentally, we adore Jesus, But we refuse to model the Kingdom values (spirit, soul, wisdom) he proclaimed and would die for again, again, and again."

Conclusion

I have attempted an understanding of the attitudes of faith, hope and charity in the light of the spiritual aspect of Adler's humanitarian psychology. In an Adlerian understanding, the spiritual attitudes of community feeling, that is, the virtues of faith, hope and charity, promote social interest. Pastors and counsellors can conceive *being faithful* as an attitude of commitment to social interest. Thus, we may understand being faithful as wholesome spiritual creativity developing a better community and a better individual. We can conceive *being hopeful* as an attitude of commitment to social interest. Being hopeful finds its realization today, not only in focussing on some future possible idealised world, but also in present existence and in the promotion of social interest. We can conceive *being charitable* as an attitude of commitment to social interest. Being charitable is striving to develop social interest among individuals living in community. Theologically, in the Christian context, being charitable can be understood as a gift received from a divine other.

From an Adlerian perspective, faith, hope and charity are methods of re-evaluation and re-direction of a lifestyle which allow exploration of new insights and personal values. This understanding can be recommended to pastors and counsellors. Practising the theological virtues brings about a loss of worry or anxiety, brings about a perception of truths not known before and brings about an apparent change in the objective appearance of the world (James, 1908).

REFERENCES

Adler, A. 1943. *Social interest: A challenge to mankind.* London: Faber & Faber

—, 1964. *Superiority and social interest: A collection of later writings* edited by H.L. Ansbacher and R.R. Ansbacher. Illinois: Northwestern University Press.

Ansbacher, H.L 1999. Alfred Adler's Concepts of Community Feeling and Social Interest and the Relevance of Community Feeling for Old Age. In *Year book 1999,* edited by P. Prina, C. Shelley and C. Thompson, 5-19. London: Adlerian Society (of the United Kingdom) and the Institute for Individual Psychology.

Brink, T.L. 1977. Adlerian theory and pastoral counselling. *Journal of Psychology and Theology*, 5: 143-49.

De Kerckhove, D. 1995. *The skin of culture: Investigating the new electronic reality.* Toronto: Somerville

Dewart, L. 1989. *Evolution and consciousness: The role of speech in the origin and development of human nature.* Toronto: Toronto University Press.

Ferré, N. 1967. *Swedish contributions to modern theology with special reference to Lundensian thought.* New York: Harper & Row.

Flannery, A. 1975. *Vatican Council II: The conciliar and post conciliar documents.* New York: Costello.

Frost, W. 1996. Directed mutations: Does it suggest vitalism? *Explorations: Journal for Adventurous Thought* 14 (4): 109-15.

Gladson, J. and R. Lucas 1989. Hebrew wisdom and psychotheological dialogue. *Zygon* 24: 357-76.

Hoffman, E. 1994. *The drive for self: Alfred Adler and the founding of Individual Psychology.* Reading, MA: Addison-Wesley.

James, W. 1908. *The varieties of religious experience.* London: Longmans, Green.

Kemp, C.F. 1947. *Physicians of the soul: A history of pastoral counseling.* New York: Macmillan.

Küng, H. 1995. *Great Christian thinkers.* New York: Continuum.

Leo XIII 1879. *Aeterni Patris.* New York: Paulist. (English text published 1951)

Lonergan, B. 1968. Renewal of religious thought. In *Renewal of religious structures*, edited by L.K. Shook, 34-46. Montréal: Palm.

Marcel, G. 1965. *Being and having: An existentialist diary.* New York: Harper

Moffatt, J. 1929. *Love in the New Testament.* London: Hodder & Stoughton.

Mosak, H. and R. Dreikurs 1967. The life tasks III. The fifth life task. *The Individual Psychologist* 5: 16-22.

Müller, A. 1992. *You shall be a blessing: Main traits of a religious humanism.* San Francisco: Alfred Adler Institute of San Francisco.

O'Connell, W. 1997. Introduction to natural high theory and practice. *The Canadian Journal of Adlerian Psychology* 27 (1): 100-122.

Rahner, K. and H. Vorgrimler. 1973. s. v. ontology. *Theological dictionary.* New York: Seaburg Press.

Shelley, C. 2000. The self of selves: An Adlerian Look at a Divisive Concept. In *Year book 2000.* P. Prina, C. Shelley and C. Thompson, 35-50. London: Adlerian Society (of the United Kingdom) and the Institute for Individual Psychology.

Slavik, S. 1994. Appreciation as a goal in Adlerian therapy. *The Canadian Journal of Adlerian Psychology* 24 (1): 47-55.

—, 1995. Editorial. *The Canadian Journal of Adlerian Psychology* 25 (2): 1-3.

—, 2000a. The idea of consciousness in Individual Psychology. *The Canadian Journal of Psychology* 30 (2) 47-63.

Slavik, S. and J. W. Croake. 1994. *Gemeinschaftsgefühl:* What it isn't and what it is. *The Canadian Journal of Adlerian Psychology* 24 (2): 1-12.

Smuts, J.C. 1926/1973. *Holism and evolution.* Westport, Conn: Greenwood.

Wuellner, B. 1966. *s v* charity, faith, hope. *A dictionary of scholastic philosophy.* Milwaukee: Bruce.

FURTHER READING

Gore-Booth, E. 1923. *A psychological and poetic approach to the study of Christ in the fourth gospel.* London: Longmans, Green.

Randall, A. 1996. Death, love, suicide, and hope: Ontological foundations for a concrete philosophy. *Explorations: Journal for Adventurous Thought* 14: 15-36.

§   §   §

Remarks Concerning Allan Savage's Article: The Spiritual Aspect of Adlerian Psychology and the Theological Virtues.

Erik Mansager

I deeply appreciate the Adlerian Year Book editors for allowing Dr. Savage and me the space to comment on one another's articles. This is a rare opportunity that I hope will stimulate further thinking on the topic of spirituality and Individual Psychology. I must express a special admiration for Dr. Savage and his journey to Adler's thinking. In his article, he applies Adlerian thought in a direct attempt at better understanding aspects of Christian moral life. This, in itself, is a recognisable act of social interest. Dr. Savage approaches, in a head-on fashion, the dualistic approach inherent in scholastic thinking. While acknowledging the importance of the traditional formulations of faith, hope and charity, he does not hesitate to point to the inherent limitation of such definitions. Scholasticism's static approach intentionally emphasises the distance between the human and its understanding of the divine. This leaves it nearly incapable of expressing the lived experience of the individual in relationship to others, and, in his view, an ultimate other.

This boldness led me to wonder what his conclusions might have been had he delved more into Adler's original thinking on spirituality rather than into those Dr. Savage considers representatives of "the Adlerian position." His references to Mosak and Driekurs (1967/2000), Müller (1954/1992), O'Connell (1997), Slavik (1994) and the particular way in which he interprets Ansbacher (1992/1999) result in what I contend is an integration of Adlerian theory and theological thought. This serves well the purpose of pastoral counselling - which was his intent. The method Adler (1933/1964) used is very different in that he does not integrate Individual Psychology with religion, but provides a collaborative critique (and in his view, a psychological correction) of Lutheran pastor Jahn's schema of human motivation or Christian anthropology.

While Dr. Savage emphasises the importance of a holistic approach to this subject matter, his integrative plan does not yet move beyond dualistic concepts. His understanding of spirituality remains, for all its Adlerian influence, one that supports a natural/supernatural dichotomy.

Without explanation, he references how "being faithful leads to .... the appreciation of that which is divine in the individual." While acknowledging that the traditional Christian image of the divine is "presently problematic," he seems content to grant such divinity a status amidst the real on the basis that "our consciousness allows that perhaps .... a divine reality really exists." He argues further that "the human mind striving within the existential situation becomes aware of another mind outside itself which it recognises as divine." Once establishing this reality-by-fiat, Dr. Savage insists that it "affectively influences our interest in community feeling;" even insisting "that which is divine and the notion of community feeling *necessarily* relate to each other." He then appeals to Adler's most recent biographer (Hoffman, 1994) as support for this dubious line of argument.

Dr. Savage is on safer ground when he observes "that which is divine, conceived as a being who has loved us first, would be rejected in Individual Psychology;" and "being faithful .... must be conceived as a relationship between the individual and another (the divine included)." These formulations point to Adler's social psychology and his appreciation for how humans construct workable fictions that promote acting "as if" certain beliefs are true. For Adler, the human being is not comprised of body and soul (or spirit) except in a metaphorical sense. Constructed apperceptions are at the root of self-bounded neurotic thinking, but they are also what bring about noble self-transcendent enterprises and undertakings when in line with the communal sense (Adler 1935). It is just this point that brings me to the reference Dr. Savage uses as the title of his stimulating article: the spiritual aspect of Adlerian psychology. This is a reference to an article wherein Ansbacher (1992/1999, 16) differentiates between community feeling and social interest. After showing social interest as "the action-line of community feeling .... for issues of self-transcendence in reference to subsocial and especially suprasocial objects, *the spiritual aspect of Adlerian psychology*" (italics added). These objects are not spiritual in the sense of "religious" or "sacred" - for which German speakers use the word *geistlich*. Rather, they are "psychical", "mental" or "intellectual" objects (both "subsocial .... such as interest in nature, art, science; and ---- suprasocial ---- such as feeling in union with life as a whole, feeling in harmony with the universe"(Ansbacher 1992/1999, 12) - for which the Germans use the adjectives *seelisch* (e.g., Adler 1933, 23) or *geistig* (e.g., Adler 1933, 29).

Dr. Savage is to be commended for his integrative work in bringing Individual Psychology to bear on theological understanding. He has provided a practical example of how Adler's thought can enrich and re-enliven religious concepts for believers today. Since Adler's understanding of humanity's self-transcendent, spiritual nature had nothing to do with another, supernatural world, Dr. Savage has shown how, precisely as such, Adler's theory is accessible to "any movement which guarantees in its final goal the welfare of all" (Adler 1933/1964, 280). Herein Adler proves to be a critical collaborator in the search for more profound understanding of the human movement towards holism and ultimate wellness.

REFERENCES

Adler, A. 1933. *Der Sinn des Lebens* [The meaning of life]. Vienna: Verlag Dr. Rolf Passer.

—, 1933/1964. Religion and Individual Psychology. In *Superiority and Social Interest. A Collection of Later Writings,* edited by H.L. Ansbacher and R.R. Ansbacher, 271-308. New York: Norton.

—, 1935. Prevention of neurosis. *International Journal of Individual Psychology* 1: 3-12.

Ansbacher, H.L. 1992/1999. Alfred Adler's Concepts of Community Feeling and Social Interest and the Relevance of Community Feeling for Old Age. In: *Year Book 1999*, edited by P. Prina, C. Shelley and C. Thompson, 5-19. London: Adlerian Society (of the United Kingdom) and the Institute for Individual Psychology.

Hoffman, E. 1994. *The drive for self: Alfred Adler and the founding of Individual Psychology*. Reading, MA: Addison-Wesley.

Mosak, H.H. and R. Dreikurs. 1967/2000. Spirituality: the fifth life task. *The Journal of Individual Psychology* 56:257-65.

Müller, A. 1954/1992. *You shall be a blessing. Main traits of a religious humanism.* San Francisco: The Alfred Adler Institute of San Francisco.

O'Connell, W. 1997. Introduction to natural high theory and practice. *The Canadian Journal of Adlerian Psychology* 27: 100-122.

Slavik, S. 1994. Appreciation as a goal in Adlerian therapy. *The Canadian Journal of Adlerian Psychology* 24: 47-55.

§   §   §

Reply to Erik Mansager's Comments on My Original Article

Allan Savage

My first impression is that Dr. Mansager has grasped and evaluated my position clearly and accurately noting what he perceives as strengths and weaknesses in my position. I do not deny that a natural/supernatural dichotomy is preserved in my theological thinking. However, it is a fictive, not actual, dichotomy. It is one that distinguishes but does not separate. This understanding is not classical dualism but, in fact, is a post-modern rational construction in which the dominant mode of reasoning is dialectical and wholistic (Kollar 2000).

Dialectical and wholistic reasoning is a said feature of lifestyle and as such it can remain relatively constant whereas it is our behaviour that changes (Meier et al 1982). Our existence, understood holistically, is greater than the sum of its constituent parts. I intend no "reality-by-fiat." I do suggest, however, that a fictive concept may have reference to another order of existence within our experience. I attempt to understand life holistically, that is, by distinguishing and deepening our appreciation of life's experiences with the assistance of Adlerian concepts.

Perhaps, at this point of critical collaboration, an artistic understanding may help distinguish the spiritual in our experience and deepen our understanding of the spiritual. Henri Bremond, of whom Tyrrell believes "his interest in religion is artistic," (Petre 1912, 265) notes: "If we say today that the poetic experience is an experience of a mystical order, or to speak more exactly, analagous to the mystical experience, we certainly irritate the latest devotees of rationalism" (Weyand 1951, 105). Theology is at home interpreting mystical experience.

Secondly, Dr. Mansager, like Adler, seems not to distinguish between "religion" and "theology." Critical collaboration is better understood, I think, not in terms of "religion" and Individual Psychology but in terms of "theology" and Individual Psychology. Religion arises out of the human practical need to make sense out of, or negotiate with, life. In this sense, religion is a means to a practical end whereas theology is a scientific approach to the interpretation of life's experiences. Like psychology, theology is an interpretive tool, not a means to a practical end. Theology, not religion, is capable of deepening our understanding of spirituality and well-being.

This distinction between religion and theology requires us to reassess Adler's statement: "The scientific nature of my work must be guarded against the hard and fast criteria of other movements which lie outside science" (Way 1956, 51). I suggest that theology lies very much inside science whereas religion does not.

The differences between Dr. Mansager and me are less pronounced in fact than in print, I am sure. I trust that our exchange is seen as contributing to a collaborative movement between Adlerian psychology and present-day theology.

REFERENCES

Kollar, N.R. 2000. Religion, identity, and three ways of life. *Explorations: A Journal for Adventurous Thought.* 19: (1) 25-41.

Meier, P., F. Minirth and F. Wichern 1982. *Introduction to Psychology and Counseling: Christian Perspectives and Applications.* Grand Rapids: Baker.

Petre, M. D. 1912. *Autobiography and life of George Tyrrell.* London: Arnold. (Vol. II.)

Way, L. 1956. *Alfred Adler: An introduction to his psychology.* London: Penguin.

Weynand, N. E. 1951. *The Catholic renascence in a disintegrating world.* Chicago: Loyola University Press.

CHAPTER 7

ESSAYS IN ADLERIAN SPIRITUALITY

Adlerian Spirituality and Stewardship in the Thinking of HRH The Prince of Wales

(The full text of the speeches may be viewed at www.princeofwales. gov.uk.)

ABSTRACT

The Prince is a visionary thinker. He seeks to discern meaning in life through understanding of individual and collective stewardship and spiritual leadership. His vision has the potential to place him among the foremost promoters of social interest in Western culture as it enters the next millennium. In tune with the times, HRH The Prince of Wales, will most likely make a positive social contribution to his country and the world. His personal spiritual journey, interpreted in terms of Adlerian principles, suggests this.

His Royal Highness has been giving speeches since 1975. Certain speeches reveal a spirituality and sense of stewardship which I examine in light of the Individual Psychology of Alfred Adler (1870-1937). Of the speeches I have selected , only a few were written for a religious occasion. The majority of them were not. However, it is on the occasion of these non-religious gatherings that the Prince shares his convictions and beliefs about spirituality and stewardship. Further, his thinking reveals a distinctive leadership style. The Prince's thinking, as reflected in his speeches, is not intended for himself alone in order to make him a better person. Rather, the prince's thinking is shared openly in the public forum for the benefit of the community. It is important that the monarch understand the spirituality that is relevant to his future subjects. By doing so he thus helps himself. If he fails, the effectiveness of monarchy in the religious life of the nation will be diminished. It is in keeping with his future role as Supreme Governor of the Church of England that he attends to common prayer and encourages spiritual growth in his future subjects. While encouraging spiritual growth does not equate to "defending the faith" one might consider the encouragement of spiritual growth as an appropriate role arising from the expectations of his future subjects. The Prince does not seem to be closed to this idea.

In personal correspondence with me, Amanda Neville, Information Officer to the Press Secretary of HRH The Prince of Wales, wrote:

> With regard to the question does His Royal Highness prepare his own speeches? Obviously His Royal Highness has a large input into the speeches, but his Private Secretaries assist along with a select band of people who are specialists in various fields. His Royal Highness obviously has the final say in the speeches that he gives.

It is difficult and somewhat risky to evaluate and draw conclusions about an individual's thoughts as they are being formed and being put into words for public presentation. Thoughts change as personality changes. Adlerian principles can serve as a guide to understanding the Prince's spiritual perspective and to recognize certain personal insights. My intent is to identify the context of his speeches, assess his words and draw conclusions about the developing spiritual philosophy of the future king of England. We will see that his visionary philosophy reveals examples of "non-competitive ways to live, including useful and desirable work and open relationships" (Croake & Slavik 1998, 72).

The Prince is convinced that seeking philosophical and spiritual meaning provides the universal link among humans. Humans seek an existential meaning that is transcendent metaphysically and/or ontologically. Mosak and Dreikurs say that, "any personal 'encounter' with God, through acceptance, alliance, public worship, individual prayer, or 'miracles' may give meaning to existence" (Mosak & Dreikurs 1967, 21). Humans strive to understand their own meaning as well as the meaning of the world that is realized by their thoughts, goals and actions. In his speeches the Prince develops transcendent notions of contributing to the common good and encouraging community participation.

The Prince is not a prophet. However, he does remind the realm, and others who care to pay attention, where and how they may have gone astray. He reminds his future subjects of eternal truths they presently seem to ignore. Drawing on personal experience that he has gained from the world that he has encountered, the Prince encourages opportunities for social improvement and supports efforts that are constructive of the human spiritual condition.

The Prince's thinking reveals a subjective and personal perspective. That is to say, he is a thinker who takes his own experience as primary. In his visionary thinking he acknowledges something, (or someone), greater than himself. He has made a decision to believe in a greater power. This, as Mosak and Dreikurs (1967) relate is part of the personal life task. Like most visionary thinkers he struggles to express himself clearly. Clues in the Prince's speeches indicate that he hopes to help others grow into a deeper understanding of spirituality and in the truth concerning the unity of objective and subjective knowledge. His way of thinking is an example of engaging in the spiritual task in life. This way of thinking will be examined under the headings: *Material and Spiritual Stewardship,* and *Spiritual Leadership.*

Material and Spiritual Stewardship

> Good stewardship celebrates the beauty and the diversity of the natural world. We should *not,* I believe, just be "managing the Earth's resources more efficiently" (relying on a traditional utilitarian ethic), but seeking to live in *balance* with the rest of creation, even if we cannot discern any direct and immediate material benefit to ourselves in that process. [1]

With these words the Prince sets an achievable goal for material and spiritual stewardship. It is his personal goal. Material and spiritual stewardship, on an individual and collective basis, are a concern for the Prince. According to him we need to recognize our individual role in conservation as well as recognizing that individuals are part of a greater whole. His holistic way of thinking accepts that the whole is greater than the sum of its individual parts.

A Marxist Socialism is not compatible with the Prince's thinking. Marxist Socialism looks only on the *material organization* of human life as the final objective of government. This denies the notion of spiritual stewardship that is arguably a proper objective of civil government. The Prince also opposes unbridled capitalism as an answer to social problems. Rather, he favours a co-operative and responsible approach to matters of material and spiritual stewardship. To further ends of material and spiritual stewardship by business and education, he suggests that:

> [A business and educational partnership] is a process which has to prepare young people for the assumption of responsibility of one kind and another, for an active approach to citizenship, and for an understanding of the spiritual and moral dimensions of life - values which are all too easily submerged in the endless search for short-term profitability or buried beneath the more debilitating aspects of consumerism. [2]

The Prince, like many in his generation, reacts to what he perceives to be an overbearing, arrogant and destructive establishment within modern society that works against the proper material and spiritual components of life. Although not a revolutionary thinker, he is an evolutionary thinker. Among his earliest memories is a horror at contemporary trends of thought that seemed aimed at "destroying the traditional foundations on which so many of our human values had been based for thousands of years." [3] These feelings the Prince had from an early age he recalls. To the Newspaper Society he says:

> qualities of understanding, tolerance, judgement and good sense...are now everywhere under attack. They seem to be threatened by pressures in our society which not only undermine these values, but also intimidate the people who hold them. It appears to me that a preoccupation with the fashionable theories and trends of the day is threatening to eat away at the values of our society. [4]

The future king has shown concern and tolerance for material stewardship by establishing various trusts. These trusts illustrate how he realizes the material and spiritual task in a pluralistic public context.

> We have to show trust, mutual respect and tolerance, if we are to find the common ground between us and work together to find solutions. The community enterprise approach of my own Trust, and the very successful Volunteers Scheme it has run for some years, show how much can be achieved by a common effort which spans the classes and religions. [5]

The material and spiritual task includes empowering stewardship within the community. Thus, those who plan urban regeneration in a society ought to seek input from that society to achieve a balance of material and spiritual benefit.

> In my experience, any approach to the problems of urban regeneration which

is not based on community participation - a participation which empowers the community - is doomed, on the whole to failure....It means helping to shift the balance of decisions from the developer and the planner towards those who live and work in a particular place. [6]

Communities are to be empowered to influence a course of urban planning to reflect an architecture of the heart.

The Millennium, according to the Prince, is a powerful visionary notion with its own creative powers for a balanced, spiritually-inspired stewardship. "We need to use the Millennium to reawaken our capacity to rejoice in all creation, to celebrate the glorious richness of God's world and to re-establish our spiritual foundations which we can draw from the great religious traditions." [7] Among the Prince's concerns disclosed through engaging in the spiritual life task is the right to worship, with a free conscience not just for Christians but non-Christians as well, as distinct from the toleration of worship. He hopes that in the moves to unite the Church of Scotland, The Scottish Episcopal Church, the United Reformed Church and the Methodists there might be ways in which the important contributions of *other churches and faiths* in Scotland can be embraced...for the good of all [italics mine].

Speaking of renewal in the Millennium he says: "This concept of renewal is not the monopoly of Christianity, but is central to many great faiths;" and, he continues to say that

the deeper, more fundamental, aspects of the Millennium are barely being considered. Why should this be when here, above all, lies so much of its true meaning and significance for us, not just as Christians, but for people of all faiths and creeds? [7]

From a societal perspective the Prince looks at the *whole* world not just the United Kingdom. His travels have given him a global perspective that is reflected in his thinking. This global outlook ensures that his thinking is not restricted to Christian interpretation. The Prince understands the Millennium as an opportunity for spiritual renewal irrespective of religious persuasion. The goals of the material and spiritual life can be presented to the nation, and the world, through the concept of Millennium renewal, he maintains.

Spiritual leadership

In the contemporary Western context little seems to be missing in life. However, according to the Prince, westerners lack a dimension of spiritual fulfilment and meaning. He writes:

> Despite all the dramatic changes that have been wrought by science and technology, and all the remarkable benefits they have indeed brought us, there remains deep in the soul (dare I mention that word?!) of mankind a persistent and unconscious anxiety that something is missing - some vital ingredient that makes life truly worth living; that provides that inexplicable sense of harmony and beauty to a world which is in danger of sacrificing these elements on the altar of an outmoded and irreverent ideology. We are told that our contemporary built environment must reflect the "spirit of the age." But what concerns me most of all is that we are succeeding in creating an "age without spirit." [3]

He addresses the Temenos Society:

> Spirituality, or a search for meaning, is the common denominator that all humans share. Spirituality is a matter of the heart, not of the head. My support for Temenos is based on the importance of maintaining perennial wisdom and traditional forms of knowledge - that is, knowledge acquired through means that come from the heart; but not necessarily from the head - (our head is so often telling us one thing, while our heart is telling us something else.) I am one of those people, for better worse, who tends to follow his heart, and that is the only way in which I can operate. I think this is an important, if hidden, feature in many people's lives, but the use of the heart is "educated out" during the process of education in the West. [8]

That our head tells us one thing and our heart another is clearly stated in a speech the Prince gave in the presence of the Salvation Army at its 1978 Congress:

> To my mind the example set by the Salvation Army is Christianity at its most essential, simple and effective level, unfettered by academic or theological concern for dogma or doctrine. In an age when we are assailed on all sides by a host of outlandish philosophies and inhuman beliefs, when people are uncertain about what is right and what is wrong and anxious about being considered old-fashioned or out of date, it seems worse than folly that Christians should still argue and bicker over doctrinal matters which only serve to bring needless unhappiness and distress to a considerable number of people. Surely what we should be worried about now is whether people are going to become atheists; whether they are going to be given an idea of what is right and wrong; whether they are going to be given an awareness of the things of the Spirit and of the meaning and infinite beauty of nature. These are the things which matter and these are the things for which Christians ought to join together with determination and understanding. [9]

Within the contemporary cultural condition, the Prince recognizes that spirituality has rights, as it were. These rights ought not to be forfeited or sold out to material concerns:

> There is, I believe, a resurgence of spirituality across the world; small beacons of civilising values in the face of the all-pervading materialism of recent times, which represent a yearning to improve the deeper quality of our lives and to restore those enduring cultural priorities which represent a moral foundation in a world dominated by consumerism. [7]

The Prince desires to provide for and aid all humanity given that all are created in God's image and likeness. This is a reflection of Alfred Adler's understanding of the purpose of religion. For the Prince, this desire to assist or aid is not merely of human origin, however. Like many Adlerian thinkers contemplating material and spiritual stewardship, the Prince recognizes another element at work prompting the living out of a peaceful existence:

> I do not expect you to agree with me, but I believe that the urgent need for western man is to discover that divine element in his being, without which there never can be any possible hope or meaning to our existence in the Earthly realm. [10]

Drawing on his personal experience, the Prince encourages opportunities for improvement and supports efforts that evoke the human spiritual condition. This leads to developing a spiritual leadership. He tells future architects:

> What I would like to be taught and explored and studied in my Institute, is the fact that the architecture that nourishes the spirit is not so much a traditional, which resembles or apes the past, but rather a particular kind of architecture whose forms, plans, materials, are based on human feeling. [3]

Later, he will go on to say of his new venture, the Foundation for Architecture and Urban Environment which brings together the work of the Phoenix Trust and Regeneration Through Heritage, that both are tackling derelict landmark heritage buildings and finding sustainable new uses for them. This is a spirituality that gives rise to a notion of stewardship based on sustainable use. The Prince leads his future subjects to collaborate with all those desiring good will who seek a vital metaphysical and/or ontological ingredient. Good will is not the preserve of Christians. For him there can be no doubt that the human condition requires not just a physical or functional sustenance, but also an emotional and a spiritual nourishment.

The Prince's speeches reveal that his understanding of personal feeling is similar to that of other Adlerian thinkers and that "one can use feeling to lead oneself into a life of community interest" (Croake & Slavik 1998, 64). The Prince encourages co-operation among his future subjects including those with contrary beliefs or no beliefs. This co-operation is an element of the spiritual task in life. Mosak and Dreikurs (1967, 17) write concerning this co-operation: "In addition to desiring God and this relationship to Him, each individual assumes a posture toward those who either do not believe in God or those who do believe in Him but who do not share the same definitions or the same forms of relating to Him."

The Prince is not a philosopher, nor an academic, nor an historian but he *is* a modern, significant thinker. His way of understanding brings the constructive thought of Adler 's way of thinking to the public forum. He says:

> I am no philosopher, but I can try to explain what I *feel* spirit to be. It is that sense, that overwhelming experience or awareness of a one-ness with the Natural World, and beyond that, with the creative force that we call God which lies at the central point of all. It is, above all, an "experience". It defies conscious thought. It steals upon you and floods your whole being despite your best logical intentions. It lies deep in the heart of mankind as if some primeval memory. It is both "pagan" *and* Christian, and in this sense is surely the fundamental expression of what we call religion. [3]

The Prince's thinking presents us with something new. He is a modern man who has shifted his thinking away from expected topics and perspectives of royal tradition and delves into an uncharted area. This shift in attitude, the break it represents with royal tradition, its warmth and fervour show a courageous development towards spirituality in the thinking of the future monarch. This engagement of material and spiritual stewardship he has truly begun on his own initiative. He explains this, in part, to future architects.

> I learnt about Descartes and scientific rationalism. I discovered that this led to a mechanistic view of the Universe and of Man's place in it and I began to realise what lay at the root of this feverish revolution....I have often wondered why it is that I was not seduced by this conveniently logical, but utterly soulless philosophical approach. [3]

This type of personal spiritual discovery is an example for all. By way of personal encouragement the Prince advises:

I would like students to learn that in order to be able to design with sensitivity and an appropriate sense of reverence for the natural surroundings, they first need to learn humility and how to submerge the inevitable egocentric tendencies that we all experience. [3]

Jonathan Dimbleby (1994), in his biography of His Royal Highness writes of a personal spiritual journey undertaken by the Prince. This journey led His Royal Highness to submerge his own, all too human, egocentric tendencies and, in turn, to suggest a way for others to follow.

REFERENCES

Croake, J. and S. Slavik. 1998. The problem of feelings. *Explorations: Journal for Adventurous Thought* 17 (2): 63-73.

Dimbleby, J. 1994. *The Prince of Wales: A biography*. Toronto: Doubleday.

Mosak, H. and R. Dreikurs, R. 1967. The life tasks III. The fifth life task. *The Individual Psychologist* 5 (1): 16-22.

Savage A. 1998. Alfred Adler's social interest: A holistic pastoral psychology. *Explorations: Journal for Adventurous Thought* 16:(3): 43-52.

SPEECHES CITED

[1] Keynote address by HRH The Prince of Wales to the World Commission on Environment and Development (The Brundtland Commission). 22 April 1992. London.

[2] Address by HRH The Prince of Wales at BITC'S Opportunity Through Partnership Exhibition. 28 October 1992. Manchester.

[3] Speech by HRH The Prince of Wales's Institute of Architecture. 30 January 1992. St James's Palace.

[4] Speech to the Newspaper Society by HRH The Prince of Wales. 4 May 1994. London.

[5] Speech by HRH The Prince of Wales on the Occasion of His Visit to the Oxford Centre for Islamic Studies. 27 October 1993.

[6] Speech by HRH The Prince of Wales to the Scottish Homes Conference. New Challenges for New Times. 27 October 1993. Glasgow.

[7] Article by HRH The Prince of Wales for *Perspectives on the Millennium*. 25 January 1996. London.

[8] Speech by HRH The Prince of Wales at the Temenos Reception at St James's Palace. 19 October 1995.

[9] Speech by HRH The Prince of Wales to the Salvation Army Congress. 30 June 1978. London.

[10] Lecture by HRH The Prince of Wales as Patron to the Royal College of Psychiatrists. 5 July 1991. Brighton.

SPEECHES CONSULTED BUT NOT REFERENCED

3 March 1975. Speech at the Parliamentary Press Gallery Luncheon. Westminster.

14 December 1982. Speech at the British Medical Association. London.

29 June 1982. Address to the British Medical Association. Dundee, Scotland.

15 July 1983. Speech at the opening of the Bristol Cancer Help Centre. Bristol.

19 December 1989. Speech given at the presentation of the Thomas Cranmer Schools Prize. St James's Church, London.

22 April 1991. Annual Shakespeare Birthday Lecture delivered by HRH The Prince of Wales. Stratford-Upon-Avon.

11 June 1992. The John Hunt Lecture given at Church House, Westminster.

10 July 1996. Remarks at the Invest Corp Dinner. London.

ADDENDUM

Within Adler's Individual Psychology, religion is a phenomenon described within social psychology. Adler did not write a great deal on religion as a phenomenon. However, his ideas are sufficiently documented to allow us to recognize a specific pattern in the behaviour of others as characterizing Adlerian thinking. By considering above various essays written by Prince Charles, I tried to discern an Adlerian posture within the thinking of the Prince. His attitude to religion as expressed in his personal sense of spirituality and stewardship, I believe, reflects this Adlerian attitude. Since 1996, the question has become: Has the Prince continued this posture in his public speeches and addresses? I answer in the affirmative. I examine some of the speeches he made from 1997 through to 2002 for his comments on spirituality and stewardship and conclude that, to date, an Adlerian perspective remains discernable in the Prince's thinking.

Spirituality

The Prince continues to speak on "inner resources" that we all possess to aid in our recovery from illness [i]. He hopes to see hospital design aid in facilitating these inner resources through which we may collectively "restore the 'soul' – the psychological and spiritual element if you like, – to its rightful place in the scheme of things" [vi]. This concern for the soul is a reflection of the civilized values inherited from our ancestors and depends on the survival of a sense of the sacred, the Prince maintains [ii]. Adler has stated that religion has fulfilled this role in the past but sees his Individual Psychology as possibly replacing religion's role. Adler is not hostile to religious activity but simply sees this replacement phenomenon as part of the evolutionary process. The Prince also notes that there is danger that our society is turning away from these values and that if not checked evolution may be heading in the wrong direction, that is, not in the interest of the community.

> It is sometimes difficult for us to appreciate this in an age when secularism has, on the one hand, weakened religions and, on the other, hardened them in the face of external threat, and turned many of their followers away from the inner and spiritual dimensions of their own religions – where alone real peace and accord reside [iii].

The danger here is that secularism works against Adler's understanding of Community Feeling. To ignore the spiritual dimension of life is to lose "an understanding of who we are and where we come from" and an "understanding of the world beyond the immediate" [v]. He admits that such religious talk is unfashionable. However, he notes that faiths other than Christian, which do not include the notion of a Creator think in "ethical" terms with respect to religious and spiritual thought [vi]. This observation gives support to Adler's notion of "God" as the most noble invention of the human mind.

H.R.H. calls for "faith" in a secular age. He notes that individuals of a given faith recognize "the faithful" of traditions other than their own [iii]. This not only happens with individuals. Communities must, also, must contribute to society as churches and faith groups strive to work together. This posture is clearly an Adlerian position. He suggests that given "the continuing role of the Church of Scotland across all aspects of Scottish society, there might be ways in which the important contributions of other churches and faiths in Scotland can be embraced in your work for the good of all" [v]. This "inclusive" attitude of religion is an understanding that Adler sees as a true and positive goal.

The Prince's faith is not juxtaposed to reason. In his thinking he does not fall into the simplistic, and erroneous understanding that there is a conflict between faith and reason. He cites Albert Einstein's close understanding between wonder and the sacred. "To him the sense of wonder was the most important sense to open ourselves to the truth, the immensity of the mystery and the Divinity of ourselves and our world" [iv]. Adler's understanding was not so much that wonder but that "the spell of religious fervor", even when seemingly not scientifically justified, brought about positive concrete results (Ansbacher & Ansbacher 1956, 462). Further, he suggests that the "the spiritual movement which results from freedom of movement is not to be undervalued" (Adler 1954, 47). Clearly, Adler's comment does not point directly to the sacred but speaks of what one might call a special appreciation of humanity. We must strive to integrate the two, the Prince concludes, so that we may live up to our goal of maintaining the trust placed in us.

> So it is only by employing both the intuitive and the rational halves of our own nature – our hearts and our minds – that we will live up to the sacred trust that has been placed in us by our Creator – or our 'Sustainer', as the ancient wisdom referred to the Creator" [vi].

Stewardship

Adler's Community Feeling is a humane and humanizing approach to life. It is not devoid of a spiritual aspect. For the Prince a mechanical or technological stewardship is not sufficient. Despite that "we are told that GM techniques will help to 'feed the world'" the Prince understands that we strive for more than temporal sophistication. Technological evolution ought to keep the perfecting of the quality of life for all individuals as a future goal [x]. We ought to make better use of existing natural resources. There is a need to create sustainable livelihoods for all since "where people are starving, lack of food is rarely the underlying cause" [xi]. Such an approach is in our community's best interest and he notes that "sustainable development is a matter of enlightened self-interest" [xiv]. This notion of "enlightened self-interest" is clearly in keeping with Adler's Individual Psychology. In fact, enlightened self-interest is a character trait in the Adlerian sense. Adler says: "The character of a human being is never the basis of a moral judgment, but is an index of the attitude of this human being toward his environment, and of his relationship to the society in which he lives" (Adler 1954, 153). In a secular age we may be seduced to rely on technology. But for technology to be of proper use "we must first of all understand that life is a more profound experience than we are told it is" [xii]. For the Prince, respect for the social environment is to be reflected in architecture. In an Adlerian manner he seeks techniques that reflect "the timeless nature of our human experience" by which he means "an architecture of the heart" [xiii]. This interest in social concerns, which is easily translated into Adler's understanding of Community Feeling, is rooted in Christian conviction. Ian Bradley notes that the Prince's interest "has deep spiritual roots and is strongly influenced by the example of Jesus Christ" (2002:134).

Adler's Community Feeling is reflected in H.R.H.'s desire to provide worship space. This desire is in opposition to the prevailing secularism of the day. The Prince writes: "The place of worship is, inevitably, a centre of community life, and remains so despite what some people would have us believe about the increasing secularism of our society" [viii]. The "centre of community life" may be understood as an Adlerian goal for which individuals strive in their lifestyle for the betterment of individual and collective life. Unlike Adler, however, the Divinity is real for the Prince, not a psychological fiction. Adler understood religion as a life-affirming social movement. God, the best invention for this purpose, is necessary for human evolutionary development. By a shift away from the traditional understanding, the Prince is prepared to be "Defender of the Divine in existence" as opposed to the traditional Defender of the faith (Bradley 2002:169). This shift in understanding is clearly in keeping with the Adlerian posture. As he strives towards this goal and recognizes that the human psyche is a unity and that "we are in fact united by a common bond of faith – faith in a sacred dimension beyond ourselves" he continues to present publically an appropriate use of Adler's Individual Psychology [vix].

SPEECHES

[i] October 21, 1997. The King's Fund Lecture on Integrated Healthcare. St James's Palace State Apartments.
[ii] April 29, 1997. Speech by HRH The Prince of Wales at the 25th Anniversary Reception for the Prayer Book Society.
[iii] July 5, 1999. King Hussein's Memorial Service. St Paul's Cathedral.
[iv] January 1, 2000. Thought for the Day: The Millennium. BBC Radio Broadcast.

[v] May 20, 2000. The Lord High Commissioner's Address to the general
Assembly of the Church of Scotland. Edinburgh, Scotland.

[vi] May 17, 2000. A Reflection on the 2000 Reith Lectures. BBC Radio
Broadcast.

[vii] November 16, 2001. Hospital Design. NHS Estates Conference at
The Prince's Foundation.

[viii] November 23, 2001. An Example To All Faiths. Launch of the
London Muslim Centre Project at the East London Mosque.

[ix] April 29, 2002. Respect Between Faiths. A Speech by The Prince of
Wales at the Launch of the Respect Campaign.

WORKS CONSULTED

Adler, A. 1954. *Understanding human nature.* New York: Fawcett.

Ansbacher, H. L. and Ansbacher, R. R. 1956. *The individual psychology
of Alfred Adler: A systematic presentation in selections from his
writings.* New York: Basic Books.

Bradley, I. *God save the queen. The spiritual dimension of monarchy.*
London: Darton, Longman & Todd.

§   §   §

Religious Belief and Adler's Social Interest

There are many psychoanalytic theories used in exploring religious belief.
Some theories have been put forward by thinkers who have a positive
view of religious belief and others who have not. Carl Rogers developed
a client-centered personality theory that is less sympathetic to religious
belief. Alfred Adler's Individual Psychology allows a role for religious
belief. Religious belief is akin to Alfred Adler's Social Interest. Social
Interest refers to a feeling of belonging, of being accepted within a
community. The German term for Social Interest is *Gemeinschaftsgefühl.*
Social Interest is more than mere civil interest or association. Social
Interest incorporates a transcendental understanding in its more developed
stages (AAISF 1997). Social Interest serves as a holistic psychology
which constitutes and distinguishes human nature from other forms of life.
Adler believed that the ultimate purpose of psychotherapy was to improve
the human social condition (Stein & Edwards 1998). This understanding

led Müller to develop a religious humanism based on Adlerian Individual Psychology (Müller 1992).

According to O'Connell (1967) writing in the New Catholic Encyclopaedia: "In Adler's theory the Christian movement represented one of the finest forces directing the movement of mankind. Its end was the search for perfection and the elevation of the family and mankind." Pioneers in the search for new philosophical ways of understanding Christian belief are Leslie Dewart and Gregory Baum. Dewart explores a new philosophic foundation for belief and Baum offers a Christian apologetic of depth experience (Dewart 1969; Baum 1969). This is significant since the traditional philosophy used by theologians to understand the forces directing the search for meaning is no longer effective for many Christians. In modern times psychological principles have been integrated into belief systems. Gladson and Lucas (1989) suggest that since Sigmund Freud and Carl Jung certain psychological and religious themes seem overworked and new ground might be explored in the psychologies of Viktor Frankl and Alfred Adler. In his defence of the psychological perspective, Lilley (1908, 97) writes:

> But it is not our fault that the philosophy of science has...shown the subjective and personal elements that contribute to the formation of abstract knowledge. So that to-day it is no longer possible to speak of a cognitive faculty which functions in complete independence of our subjective needs and interests, and arrives at a certainty and a truth which is 'an equation of thought to thing' (*adaequatio rei et intellectus*).

A contemporary holistic psychological understanding is needed to replace traditional philosophical understanding. Ellison and Smith (1991, 35) state that "holistic conceptions of healthy personality and functioning are an integral part of the personality theories of Adler, Allport, Maslow, and Rogers." Holistic understanding is a non-classical approach to belief in a living organism which "has a reality other and greater than the sum of its constituent parts" (Funk & Wagnalls, 1989).

Adler's ideas can be successfully integrated into belief systems but psychologists are loathe to discuss them (Mosak & Dreikurs 1967). Adler's Social Interest facilitates construction of a belief system and as a holistic approach it provides a new vehicle for spiritual meaning.

Alfred Adler, who was Jewish-born, converted to Protestantism in later life but not out of religious conviction (Hoffman 1994). Even so, Hoffman notes that Adler collaborated with the Lutheran pastor, Ernest Jahn, in a religious work entitled, *Religion and Individual Psychology*. However, Adler himself remained independent and neutral "as towards the efforts of Catholic or Protestant psychologists to combine [his] views with religious doctrine" (Hoffman 1994, 194).

Adler's Social Interest is shaped through participation in life and not merely by the observation of life. Therefore, it is an existential psychology. Adler's existential psychology is among those non-scholastic holistic belief systems that are helpful to spiritual understanding. The reasons for this are discussed below.

1st Reason: Individual Psychology is a positive approach

The first reason to accept Adler's Individual Psychology as helpful is its positive approach to life and its support of a spiritual understanding. In secular (humanist) psychologies, particularly dominant in the United States, religious understanding of life is often seen to require some form of corrective intervention by psychologists. Adler's understanding of Social Interest is a highly effective tool that is at the "level of preventive rather than corrective intervention" (Bishop 1989, 155). All too often, in the dominant secular culture of the West, to account for a religious belief in psychological terms is seen as something negative, as a crisis to be overcome or solved in one's life. However, a historian of American political thought writes of a shift in this understanding. Butler (1997) says that there is a large body of critical scholarship that challenges this idea.

Corrective intervention may be seen as a reaction to Freud's view of religion in *The Future of the Illusion*. Sorenson (1990) counters Freud's negative position. In Sorenson's view the struggle to express belief in life in psychological terms is accepted as a positive act, that is to say, as preventive intervention, not corrective intervention. Preventive intervention comprises part of the normal stages of growth and development of each individual (McMinn & Lebold, 1989).

Systems of belief address important life tasks for the betterment of the individual and society. As Adler phrases it: "We approach the problem from a different angle but the goal is the same--to increase interest in others" (Adler 1931, 12). Alfred Adler's Individual Psychology stresses the importance of positive nurturing within the environment. Stein and Edwards (1998) explain that the goal of therapy is to increase the feeling of community, to promote a feeling of equality and, as well, to replace an egocentric self-protection and self-indulgence with a self-transcending, courageous and social contribution. In this way an individual attains health and becomes helpful within a community and society.

2nd Reason: Individual Psychology relates to the current context

The second reason to accept Individual Psychology as helpful to a belief system is that it corresponds to contemporary spiritual understanding. Western Christians do not live in a classical world. Classical philosophy is often of little value to individuals in coping in their day-to-day lives. I am not the first, nor indeed the last, to recognize that classical philosophy is no longer adequate for the contemporary context. William James came to the same conclusion. In an attempt to show the contrary, that classical understanding was indeed adequate for contemporary understanding, James wrote *The Varieties of Religious Experience* (James 1908). What resulted, however, was the realization on his part that psychology was better suited than philosophy to interpret religious understanding in modern times. James (1908, 455) concludes:

> Philosophy in this sphere [of religious belief] is thus a secondary function, unable to warrant faith's veracity....In all sad sincerity I think we must conclude that the attempt to demonstrate by purely intellectual processes the truth of the deliverances of direct religious experience is absolutely hopeless.

Adler discusses the idea of God as a product of spiritual meaning in *Social Interest: A Challenge to Mankind.* He says: "The best conception hitherto gained for the elevation of humanity is the idea of God....The primal energy which was so effective in establishing regulative religious goals was none other than that of social feeling" (Adler 1943, 272). Social Interest is a way of understanding belief that is appropriate to our times. It reflects a spiritual understanding arising from our experience that cannot be expressed through classical thinking, but only existentially.

3rd Reason: Individual Psychology promotes communal relationships

Adler's Individual Psychology is a helpful perspective for spiritual understanding in that it reinforces the communal relationship of the individual in society. It does not encourage individualism. In Individual Psychology, "individuality" is not to be confused with "individualism." The latter is concerned with a distinct theory or doctrinal system that reflects a classical way of thinking, whereas the former is concerned with one's state, condition or quality of life which reflects a phenomenological way of thinking. O'Connell, an Adlerian interpreter, speaks of Adler's psychology as promoting the "individuated" person rather than the "individual" person. He states that individuated psychology speaks of a deep eternal Self, as well as broad social concerns. This deep eternal Self and its broad social concerns describe human understanding and make it possible to articulate a belief system.

In Summary

Human growth consists of positive nurturing in a belief system. Individual Psychology consists of basic orientations that are supportive of human growth. These orientations are 1) that all important life problems are social, that is, they beset the individual in a social context; 2) that health is attained by the individual in a set of harmonious social relationships.

Health and well-being are fundamental to a spiritual lifestyle. They can be, to a great extent, attained through harmonious social relationships. The spiritual life style, which seeks health and seeks to prevent illness (physical and spiritual), must be lived out in community.

Formal ways of thinking have tended to view health and well-being from a classical perspective. This understanding is no doubt due to the persistent reliance on classical Greek philosophical thinking typified by Plato and Aristotle. Currently, Individual Psychology criticizes this classical and static way of thinking: "The human spirit is only too well accustomed to reduce everything that is in flux to a form, to consider it not as movement but as frozen movement--movement that has become form" (Adler 1943, 269). While form is an acceptable interpretation in a classical school of thought, it is not an acceptable within a belief system arising from contemporary experience.

REFERENCES

Adler, A. 1931. *What life should mean to you.* New York: Blue Ribbon Books.

—, 1943. *Social Interest: A challenge to mankind.* London: Faber & Faber.

Alfred Adler Institute of San Francisco. 1997. *Twelve Stages Classical Adlerian Psychotherapy.* http://www.behavior.net/orgs/adler/principle.html.

Baum, G. 1969. *Faith and doctrine: A contemporary view.* New York: Newman Press.

Bishop, D. 1989. Psychology and the pastoral ministry: Help or hindrance? *Journal of Psychology and Theology* 17: 151-56.

Butler, G. 1997. Visions of a nation transformed: Modernity and ideology in Wilson's political thought. *Journal of Church and State* 39: 35-51.

Dewart, L. 1969. *The foundations of belief.* New York: Herder & Herder.

Ellison, C. and J. Smith. 1991. Toward an integrative measure of health and well-being. *Journal of Psychology and Theology* 19: 35-48.

Funk and Wagnalls. 1989. *Canadian College Dictionary, sv* holism. Toronto: Fitzhenry & Whiteside.

Gladstone, J. and R. Lucas. 1989. Hebrew wisdom and psychotheological dialogue. *Zygon* 24: 357-76.

Hoffman, E. 1994. *The drive for self: Alfred Adler and the founding of Individual Psychology.* Reading, MA: Addison-Wesley.

James, W. 1908. *The varieties of religious experience: A study in human nature.* London: Longmans Green.

Lilley, L. 1908. *The Programme of modernism: A reply to the encyclical of Pius X.* New York: Putnam.

McMinn, M. and C. Lebold 1989. Collaborative efforts in cognitive therapy with religious clients. *Journal of Psychology and Theology* 17: 101-09.

Mosak, H. and R. Dreikurs 1967. The life tasks III: The fifth life task. *The Individual Psychologist* 5: 16-22.

Müller, A. 1992. *You shall be a blessing: Main traits of a religious humanism.* San Francisco: Alfred Adler Institute.

O'Connell, W 1997. Introduction to natural high theory and practice. *Canadian Journal of Adlerian Psychology* 27: 100-122.

Sorenson, A. 1990. Psychoanalytic perspectives on religion: The illusion has a future. *Journal of Psychology and Theology* 18: 209-17.

Stein, H. and M. Edwards. 1998. Alfred Adler: Classical Theory and Practice. In *Psychoanalytic Versions of the Human Condition: Philosophies of Life and Their Practice,* edited by P. Marcus and A. Rosenberg, 64-93. New York: New York University Press.

§   §   §

Wholism or Holism in Individual Psychology and Theology

ABSTRACT

Psychologists and theologians use the terms *wholism* and *holism* in discussing the individual in a secular and/or religious context. The works of certain Adlerian psychologists show that the terms are neither used nor understood in any conventional manner by these authors. A conventional use of these terms by Adlerian psychologists and phenomenologically-minded theologians could assist in establishing a collaborative approach to understanding the individual in a secular and/or a religious context.

In academic discussions it is necessary to distinguish between speculative and qualitative language. Speculative language belongs to classical philosophy, whereas qualitative language belongs to phenomenological philosophy. The suffixes "-ism" and "-ity" reflect this distinction. Funk and Wagnall's Canadian College Dictionary (1989) defines "-ism" as a suffix attached to nouns to mean "a distinctive theory, doctrine, or system: usually used disparagingly;" "-ity" is a suffix attached to nouns to mean a "state, condition, or quality." The following pairs of terms, often used in discussions in philosophy, theology and psychology conform to this distinction: *personalism* versus *personality*, *humanism* versus *humanity*, *nationalism* versus *nationality*, *historicism* versus *historicity*, *Catholicism* versus *Catholicity*, *individualism* versus *individuality*, *spiritualism* versus *spirituality*, *modernism* versus *modernity*, *dualism* versus *duality*, *rationalism* versus *rationality*, *moralism* versus *morality* and *Deism* versus *Deity*. Words ending in "-ity" reflect a phenomenological philosophical language, whereas "-ism" words reflect a speculative philosophical language.

The notions of *wholism* and *holism* provide a focal point to ponder over this distinction within Adler's Individual Psychology and theology. To ask whether or not the terms wholism and holism, although both ending in "-ism," are distinguished in the same fashion as many other words ending in "-ism" and "-ity" helps us to understand how the terms are used in Individual Psychology and theology. Frost (1997, 68) thinks the terms can be differentiated and distinguishes between wholism (a unit) and holism (a unity). He suggests we would do well

> not to confuse wholism with holism. Wholism emphasises the importance of the whole in the study of its parts. Whatever exists is part of a greater whole that influences the nature of the part. This is a scientific concern....Holism, it seems, is less into scientific methodologies. It is more an awareness about monistic aspects of existence, contrary to dualistic views.

Holism, being more concerned with monistic aspects, the state or quality of entities, belongs more properly to the intent of the "-ity" list of words, whereas, wholism belongs to the "-ism" list of words, Frost would argue.

This distinction, however, is not supported by Corsini (1999). In the *Dictionary of Psychology,* he notes that the term "holism" derives from the thinking of J. C. Smuts and he seems to understand that "wholism" is but an infrequent spelling of holism. To Corsini, it seems, the terms mean the same. In this essay I examine the understanding and usage of the terms. I do not examine the correctness of the conclusions drawn from their usage.

Smuts and Holism

Smuts (1927) discusses the notion of what he describes as the Supreme Whole in *Holism and Evolution.* He does include the notion of the Christian God in his discussion. In reply to Msgr Kolbe (1928, vii/viii) he writes:

> This, of course, is an aspect of Holism which is not touched upon in my book. I was there trying to lay the foundations of the idea; I was trying to build the new structure from its foundations. The Religious Ideal, like the other great Ideals and Values of the spirit, is not yet reached in my treatment of Holism, although, to be sure, the understanding reader will find more in the book than is actually written there.... Within the limited scientific purview of the book I do not discuss God, as such a discussion would in my opinion have been out of place in such a context.

As well, Kolbe (1928, 51) is clear in his intent.

> Hitherto, I have been considering not what General Smuts has expressly put forward as his theory, but what the Catholic student should have in his own mind while studying that theory. I fully believe that a great deal of what I have been 'reading into' this book is implicitly contained therein; and I want Catholic students to read it from that point of view. It is not a usual point of view. That is to say, General Smuts, writing for scientists and natural philosophers, is silent on certain topics, and in our ordinary experience such silence usually indicates antagonism. It is not so here. The aim of the whole book is spiritual, not materialistic.

Smuts discusses the nature of the Supreme W hole [holism] as a way of exploring philosophically the notion of that which may reflect the divine in human consciousness. In other words, the Supreme Whole is Smuts's phenomenological view which replaces what the speculative theologians understand as Deism. Smuts, phenomenologically understood, in fact, is discussing Deity. Smuts (1927, 347) poses this question: "In other words, is there a Whole, a Supreme Whole, of which all lesser wholes are but parts or organs?" Here, Smuts is struggling to express relationships that are open to the transcendent. The fundamental phenomenological task is to express the relationship among wholes and the Supreme Whole such that the expression overcomes the dichotomy of speculative thinking between the knower and the known, creature and creator. To his mind, this question must be considered because his argument for a Supreme Whole "implies clearly something more to complete it" (Smuts 1927, 347). For the speculative theologian, however, the question is: Is this "something more" to be equated with God? Further, Smuts (1927, 349) says "nature is holistic without being a real whole." In saying this, it seems to me, that Smuts is trying to say that there is nothing greater outside nature. Nature itself is all-encompassing. This notion challenges theologians and psychologists schooled in a speculative way of thinking. McCool (1977, 12) offers a phenomenological (non-speculative) perspective by which to ponder the notion of Smuts's Supreme Whole. He says:

> In post-Kantian philosophy, . . . the Infinite Absolute went out of itself through its finite self-manifestation in the dynamic universe of nature and spirit. . . . In the same way, each natural human community in the spiritual universe had its own specific communal idea that achieved the perfection of its realisation through the free activity of individual members. And, since spiritual realities were also self-conscious, the community's formative idea manifested itself on the level of consciousness as the communal spirit or *Geist*.

By abandoning speculative thinking, McCool conceives the transcendent and the immanent as co-terminus, that is, they form a unity, distinguishable but not separable with respect to their internal relationships. Phenomenological understanding presents some challenges concerning relationships for speculative thinkers. Phenomenological understanding is the forum in which Adler's thinking operates. The authors represented below, like McCool, whose Infinite Absolute "went out of itself," discuss wholism and holism without taking into account the classical concept of revelation. As a result, they can only discuss God as "a God of the philosophers," that is, an objective God of reasoned thought and not as the God of personal revelation. Smuts (1927, 350) suggests that a God that is a product of the natural process of human understanding is not a worthy object of worship. He writes: "The belief in the Divine Being rests, and necessarily must rest, on quite different grounds, as a God whose concept is deduced from natural process is not a being whom the human soul can worship."

According to Smuts (1927, 353), whose thinking it seems is similar to

McCool's, the psychologist's notion of Deity and not the speculative philosopher's concept of Deism is more acceptable to contemporary thought. He continues:

> The holistic nisus which rises like a living fountain from the very depths of the universe is the guarantee that failure does not await us, that the ideals of Well-being, of Truth, Beauty and Goodness are firmly grounded in the nature of things, and will not eventually be endangered or lost. . . . The rise and self-perfection of wholes in the Whole is the slow but unerring process and goal of this Holistic universe.

His thinking seems to be influenced by that of the English metaphysician Samuel Alexander (1859-1938). Alexander apparently conceived the deity as the next highest level to be emerged out of any given level. Thus for beings on the level of life, mind is deity, but for beings possessing minds there is a *nisus* or urge toward a still higher quality. To such beings that dimly felt quality is deity. The quality next above any given level is deity to the beings on that level. For humans, deity has not yet emerged, but there is a *nisus* towards its emergence (Runes 1963,8). Smuts uses the term holistic and conceptualizes his thinking phenomenologically thus distinguishing it from speculative philosophical conceptualizations. This distinction must be left to phenomenological philosophers and theologians for further exploration within human relationships. But are there any clues as to how this distinction is currently appreciated?

Recent Adlerian Thinking

Adlerian psychologists use notions of wholism and holism, or they discuss notions in terms of the social field that incorporates an understanding of wholism or holism. In this essay I ponder how some psychologists seem to understand these terms. Judging by the way in which the terms wholism and holism are used there seems to be no standardized acceptance of the terms according to either Frost's understanding or Corsini's definition.

Vande Kemp (2000), for example, does not mention wholism or holism in her article. The title of her article, however, "Wholeness, holiness, and the care of souls: The Adler-Jahn debate in historical perspective," invites consideration from a wholistic versus holistic perspective. The care of souls, which involves the acquisition of a strong, God-focussed sense of destiny in a person's life, is more satisfactorily articulated in terms of a phenomenological understanding of wholism and holism than in the speculative view of Christian/secular anthropologies which she discusses (Vande Kemp 2000, 243). A phenomenological (wholistic/holistic) understanding of the question would remove the dichotomy between, or dissociation of, Christian soul-care and secular soul-care of the person between the thinking of Adler and Jahn that Vande Kemp has identified.

It is worth taking further note of her understanding of this relationship. From a collaborative viewpoint I asked her to respond to the following statement:

> Rather than think in terms of two compatible disciplines being integrated with respect to anthropological and ontological assumptions, we would do well to make unified anthropological and ontological assumptions about the individual and subsequently understand the person from a psychological and theological aspect of being. In other words, the focus is on the person, not the disciplines.

In her reply, she indicated that she prefers to remain focussed on the disciplines, not the person, which she seems to understand as not existing outside a social field. Her thinking would, I suspect, fall into the camp that recognizes wholism as the preferred context of understanding the person. She answered: "I would say an adequate psychology can only be focussed on Persons-in-Relation, to borrow a phrase from the British philosopher John Macmurray." A focus on the person, she seems to suggest, would be a focus on what is only a hypothetical situation, a whole. Her thinking seems to be somewhat parallel to Noda's (2000) approach discussed below.

In their article, "Spirituality: Life task or life process," Gold and Mansager (2001, 274) write that "the German root word *Geistig*, can be legitimately translated 'spiritual' but has the restricted sense of 'mental' or 'intellectual.' To convey 'spiritual' in the sense of 'religious' or 'sacred' Germans use the word *geistlich*. The term *geistlich* does not appear in Adler's s German text." They beg the question of distinguishing between wholism and holism in their understanding of Individual Psychology and theology. Can the term *geistig* be understood in the wholistic sense and *ghostlike* in the holistic sense? To illustrate, I insert these terms in square brackets into Mansager's reply to my question: Is it correct, based on your explanation of the terms *'geistig'/'geistlich'*, to draw the conclusion that they can be considered more as theological terms than psychological terms? In reply, Mansager says:

> maybe we need to distinguish clearly between the terms theological and psychological. I think they weren't so separate once upon a time. . . . And

the split developed into 'geistig' as the intellectual freedom of humanity [wholism] and 'geistlich' as the sacred [holism]--both get at the 'principle of life.' The first from the psychological or mental/intellectual and the second from the religious. Need these be at odds? . . . Does one have a greater reality than the other? I answer in the negative.

I agree with his position. Both theology and psychology are interpretative tools and it is of no benefit to think in terms of one being greater than the other. Mansager continues:

I contend that we can approach this secular world and understand it . . . as sacred from any number of perspectives (Catholic richness having much to offer), but the secular basis is what we are commenting on [wholism]. It is this basis that the Buddhist and Muslim can also comment on.

To my mind, thinking as a theologian, I recognize the personal (holistic) basis, before the secular (wholistic) basis, as the focus which the Buddhist and Muslim comment on. The human being in a holistic social field is what ought to capture our attention. The person, understood within a holistic social field, admits of no qualitative distinction or preferential consideration. Theologically, in a popular manner, we say "all persons are equal in the eyes of God." The means or the tools to understand the person are, however, a secondary consideration and do admit of distinction and preference.

The distinction between psychology and theology, as tools, arises only after the scientific age is upon us as Mansager has correctly noted. But, I contend, for Western-style thinking that no possibility exists of returning to an earlier way of thinking when both disciplines were effectively seen as one. The scientific method, a product of the Western intellect, will most likely effectively prevent this from happening. With respect to philosophical collaboration in Occidental and Oriental thinking, Ross (1912, 356) writes: "Equipped with that incomparable instrument, *the scientific method* [author's emphasis], the Western intellect will probably go on its way with little heed to what the East offers it." The scientific method is the Western contribution to the world and we cannot turn back the clock. In order of personal consciousness within the social field, first arises psychology (a catholic human science), then theology develops (a catholic sacred science). These are able to collaborate with each other. Such collaboration leads to an understanding of the "principle of life" that transcends human nature. In this sense Tyrrell (1963/1909, 2) conceives of Christianity as the highest spontaneous development of the religious Idea and, therefore, the religion most capable of reflective development, in the light of a science of religion gleaned from historical and psychological investigation, i.e. most capable of becoming as catholic and perpetual as that science.

Psychology talks about the order of nature and Christian theology talks about the order of grace. This distinction between psychology (a wholistic enterprise) and theology (a holistic enterprise) is within the emergence of human understanding and, as a result, is not reversible. Rather than regress, our understanding of psychology and theology must evolve collaboratively and distinctively converging on an understanding of the person. Frost's understanding, discussed above, seems to be reflected in Gold and Mansager's article.

Ellis offers another perspective. He is an acknowledged secular humanist. His thinking about wholistic versus holistic perspectives in therapeutic treatment is revealed in his statement: "Even if the therapist is, as I am, a secular humanist and does not personally believe in anything supernatural, transcendental, or higher-than-human, such beliefs can sometimes be used" (Ellis 2000, 282). I understand Ellis as writing within Corsini's definition that makes no distinction between wholism and holism. In a similar vein, Brinton (1876:iii), a medical doctor who earlier studied the religions of the native race of America, a field he selected as most favourable by reason of the simplicity of many of it cults, and the absence of theories respecting them, has this to say regarding the distinction to be made between human and non-human life. Briton (1876, 8) notes:

> The distinction between the animal and vegetable worlds, between the reasoning and unreasoning animals, is one of degree only. Whether, in a somewhat different sense, we should not go yet further, and say that the mind is co-extensive with motion, and hence with phenomena, is a speculative inquiry which may have to be answered in the affirmative, but it does not concern us here.

Brinton then develops his thinking along a psychological understanding that is particular to humans. Brinton might see in Ellis a reflection of his own understanding. Ellis (2000, 280) states:

> having a profound belief that all beings, animate and inanimate, are holistically interconnected and integrated is realistic to some degree--because humans depend on other animals and on an inanimate environment and could not remain alive without them. If people believe, however, that plants and trees are as alive as they are--as some followers of Lao-Tsu believe--they are

probably quite unrealistic, will refuse to use animals and objects for their healthy purposes, and will hardly survive.

To those with a spiritual sensitivity or compassionate religious outlook, Ellis's conclusion might seem to be harsh. However, there is a Biblical theological interpretation that does help with Ellis's pragmatic understanding. In Genesis, the world order before the flood is contrasted with the world order after the flood. *A New Catholic Commentary on Holy Scripture* (1969:187) reads:

> God recognises as the *status quo* fallen man in a disordered world that has replaced the paradisiacal peace of the first creation. Therefore, permission is given for the eating of flesh, provided that the sanctity of life is still recognised.

Ellis (2000, 280) writes from a perspective that seems, at first, to reduce the possibility of theological and psychological collaboration:

> Having a meaning or purpose in life that is outstanding or greater than oneself--what Tillich called ultimate concern and Frankl called purposeful meaning--may be good for most people most of the time, but it may not be good for all people all of the time.

Ellis's critique of meaning and purpose has a parallel in the theological thinking of George Tyrrell (1861-1909), who also believed that "too much religion is not a good thing," as it were. Regretfully, the controversy surrounding him in his day obscured the originality and insight of his theological thought. Within a theological, not psychological, understanding Tyrrell came to the same conclusions as Ellis concerning a purposeful meaning in life. When meaning in life is inhibited by church structure, Tyrrell (1906, 86/100) writes:

> For, after all, the visible church (unlike the invisible) is but a means, a way, a creature, to be used where it helps, to be left where it hinders. . . . [I speak of] the immense variety of means which [the Church] offers for our help--some for the use of all; all for the use of none.

From another point of view, Noda's interpretation of Adler, who is a Teutonic thinker, incorporates Buddhist philosophical thinking. In the abstract to Noda's article, "The concept of holism in Individual Psychology and Buddhism," we read: While Buddhism applies holism to understanding the structure of the universe, Individual Psychology recognises conflicts between the individual and the world (Noda 2000,

285). Further, Noda understands absolute holism to be equivalent to Adler's notion of Social Interest. He accepts that there is a distinction, but not a separation, to be made between wholism and holism. His perspective is in keeping with Frost's understanding, not Corsini's definition.

It is worth noting that Wenfeng and Shaojie (1991, 152) offer explanation and support for Noda's distinction of wholism and holism. They write:

Chinese philosophers' mental structures are integrated ones, unsophisticated and comprehensive. They underline the unity of the self and the indivisibility of the internal spiritual structure of the subject. . . . In reality human life, knowledge, feeling and will are organically unified. There is neither isolated, pure speculation nor isolated feelings and will. People may divide them through abstraction in their minds. But they cannot do so in reality.

In Eastern philosophy there is no basis, or underlying equivalent reality to the Western notion of ego or "I," in understanding the person. There is, however, some variation in how the individual is understood within Eastern philosophical thought. On the subject of an "I" in the Western sense, Wenfeng and Shaojie (1991, 161) write:

Most Chinese philosophers affirm the identity of the subject and object. But their differences become evident if they are asked whether their identity is differential or non-differential. These differences may be found in and between Confucianism, Taoism and Buddhism. Confucianists from the Lu-Wang school and Buddhists from the Chan school are for non-differential identity. Among Confucianists, those from the Lu-Wang school are for non-differential identity while those from the Cheng-Zhu school are for differential identity.

Upon noting the diagrams in Noda's article depicting the concepts of Pluralism, Monism and Holism, I inquired of him about Frost's distinction between wholism and holism. He replied:

I use the word 'holism' exactly in the same meaning to the quotation. Last year, I discussed with Dorothy Peven in Chicago about this problem. She insisted that the Adlerian 'holism' just meant that there was no conflict between parts of the mind. I objected to her and told her that it was an 'organismic' or 'systematic' view of the individual, which denied the concept of the 'self' as a main part of the mind. This October, Bernard Shulman came to Japan, and I discussed with him. He often used the word 'self,' but we were able to agree with each other. He accepted my idea that the 'self' was a fiction. Referring to the constructivism, he said to me, I would like to say that we behave 'as if' the self actually exists.

Noda (2000, 292) distinguishes between "relative holism" and "absolute holism" and writes "there is no conflict between the individual and the world" in absolute holism. I would suggest, however, from a Western theological point of view that not an "absence of conflict" notion, but a "greater than the sum of its parts" notion is more appropriate in distinguishing relative holism from absolute holism, or rather distinguishing wholism from holism. Since Noda's conclusion does not include the "greater than the sum of its parts" notion which characterizes holism, he seems, in effect, to have understood absolute holism as wholism.

Cheston, by introducing an ontological perspective into her argument favours Frost's notion of wholism and holism. In "Spirituality of encouragement" Cheston (2000) roots her understanding of holism and wholism in Smuts's thinking and comments that Smuts's holism is an ontology to express the view that the ultimate reality of the universe is neither matter nor spirit but wholes. In a reply to my question about the distinction between holism/wholism, she answered: "I have always agreed that there is a difference between holism and wholism." Her understanding of the term holism opens the way for a collaborative relationship between psychology and theology in that encouragement is a bridge between the outer and inner worlds of an individual. She says: "I think that everyone wants to think of spirituality as a counseling issue but few want to acknowledge God in the middle of it so they gravitate to the word wholism."

Further, she maintains the possibility of the ongoing interpretation of an original thinker's initial notions. Her article supports the Adlerian fifth life task. Cheston (2000, 301) writes:

> The belief in a transcendent being or energy that causes a person to relate to the cosmos, God, or universal values was a fifth life task that Adler alluded to in his writings and that has been more clearly defined by Mosak and Dreikurs.

Gold and Mansager (2000, 275) suggest otherwise, however, and retain only three Adlerian life tasks. My question to Cheston was:

> In light of Gold and Mansager's article, 'Spirituality: Life Task or Life Process,' from your perspective, is there less reason to develop Adler's thinking specifically with reference to a spiritual fifth life task?

She replied:

> As far as [this] question is concerned, I do believe that we must keep
> exploring Adlerian's notions of the fifth task and incorporate spirituality as
> the fifth life task. Jungians agree, too.

Theologians, like psychologists, face the same historical problem. Can
the initial ideas or notions of theologians sustain further development by
their followers? Weaver cites the example of Thomas Aquinas (died 1274)
and Suarez (1548-1617). Suarez interpreted scholastic thinking along
lines on which St. Thomas himself would most likely not agree. In fact,
Weaver (1981, 11) notes that Suarez departed from Aquinas on some
issues and some scholars discern Suarezism as a system of its own, even
in competition with that of Aquinas. Psychologists are in the same
position. Would the initiator of a psychological school of thought (Adler)
agree with current developments carried out by contemporary disciples?
Only time shows how faithfully and successfully contemporary thinkers
interpret innovative thinkers in theology and psychology.

Watts's operational definition and characteristics of healthy Christian
spirituality fit into Frost's description of wholism and holism. In his
article, "A Biblically based spirituality," Watts, (2000) reminds us of the
role of revelation in theology. Revelation is problematic for Adlerians. The
Adlerian view purports to be scientific but Watts (2000, 320) connects
Christian revelation (theology) and Individual Psychology such that "It
appears that Jesus is stating that the focus of God's revelation addresses
how people are to be in relationship to God [holism] with their fellow
human beings [wholism]." Watts's notions reflect a monistic, not
scientific, understanding. He accurately understands Individual
Psychology and biblical spirituality as able to conceptualize humans as
creative, holistic, socially oriented, and teleologically motivated (goal-
directed) (Watts 2000, 319).

Individual Psychology and biblical theology can work collaboratively
to the benefit of the believing client. "If they do indeed view the Bible as
the Word of God, then facilitating a dialogue between the Bible and their
maladaptive beliefs and behaviours often proves helpful" (Watts 2000,
325). After reading Watts's article I asked him the following question
about the terms wholism and holism.

> While you do not use the terms, it seems to me, unless I have misread your
> position, that in your thinking you intend to transcend those categories. The
> understanding of God in biblically based Christian spirituality is not
> equivalent to Adler's idea of God, which is a social construction (a fiction).

If holism/wholism is interpreted from an Adlerian point of view there is no admitting that a personal God (Spirit of God) exists outside one's consciousness. Am I correct in my interpretation here with respect to your position?

His reply supports the thinking of Cheston discussed above.

In terms of the Adlerian position on holism/wholism, it appears to me that the definition of spirituality set forth by Mosak and Dreikurs is sufficiently broad to allow Adlerians to espouse a personal God-centred holism or a pantheistic (or polytheistic) perspective on holism. Although the philosophical underpinnings of each contain significant differences, the focus on viewing humans as holistic or indivisible beings remains similar.

There is a possibility of a new understanding of the transcendent in the immanent within Adlerian psychology or because of Adlerian psychology. Rather than interpret the Deity pantheistically, we may understand the notion of the transcendent as being within the immanent. This requires a phenomenological understanding, not a speculative interpretation. A phenomenological understanding is required to realize a God-centred holism. Adler's understanding can help us grow out of a pantheistic mind-set even though Adler conceived God only as a useful fiction.

Like Cheston, Watts uses the potential of Adlerian thinking to develop the understanding of spirituality beyond the three stages to which Gold and Mansager limit Adler's notions. Watts's purpose is to show how Adlerian thinking is amenable to working with clients who subscribe to a Biblical understanding of spirituality.

Slavik (2000) begs the question of wholism and holism from within an Adlerian understanding in his article, "The subject matter of Individual Psychology." In his discussion he addresses the idea of persons conceived by Adler as units [wholes]. Slavik accepts Smuts's understanding that a social field is a subjective reality limited to the inner area of a conscious individual. Slavik makes distinctions that can be understood to be referring to a conscious individual [wholisticallly understood] within a social field [holistically understood]. The person is: "The active element in the social field, the entity that interacts meaningfully in the field with others, that is in motion, directed and purposive organized and with goals. The person does not exist outside of the field" (Slavik 2000, 39).

The relationship that exists between the person and the social field is such that one notion cannot exist without the other. In this understanding, the distinction between wholism and holism is problematic for the psychologist and theologian. Does a person's social field comprise the sum total of reality? If so, ought it not be considered wholistic, not holistic? Also, if the social field determines the personality, what is determined by a collection of social fields?

In addressing these questions theologians are tempted to appeal to revelation, to something outside the social field, to their understanding of the constitution of the person as a whole. Does a collection of wholes become a social field implying an Absolute Whole? In this understanding some theologians may consider the notion of the "person" of God being co-terminus with the social field (an Adlerian notion). In the minds of most Christian theologians, however, this is pantheistic thinking and unacceptable. Could a holistic way of thinking include immanence and transcendence, in a non-dualistic way of understanding? In Christian theology, a strong existential argument resists the acceptance of God restricted to a social field. Being restricted to a social field is tantamount to a denial of revelation.

In reply to my question: "Does consciousness arise in the social field?" Slavik wrote: "consciousness requires a social field to come into being. . . . So the social field is necessary for consciousness to develop." The consciously creative person selects values from the social field through which he or she is created. This seems to situate Slavik's thinking, theologically speaking, in the nineteenth-century German idealist's perspective. Dulles (1969, 62) writes that idealist philosophical and historical thinking has re-structured theological ways of thinking.

> The nineteenth century presents an extremely rich development of the history of revelation under the stimulating impact of idealistic philosophy on the one hand and of historical thinking on the other. Idealist philosophy, rebelling against the narrowness of eighteenth century Rationalism, discovered the Absolute in a new way. Historical thinking, on the contrary, made theologians conscious of the cultural relativity of their ideas about God.

This restructuring of thinking opens the way for collaboration between psychology and theology.

Conclusion

Critical collaboration, I suggest, a notion first suggested to me by Mansager (2001), requires that psychologists study theologians and that theologians study psychologists along the lines of Lilley's thinking. Smuts lays a foundation for thinking phenomenologically, not speculatively, about wholism and holism. Through the notions of wholism and holism I presented a reflection on the thinking of various Adlerian psychologists. The following is a summary of my fledgling attempt at critical collaboration as a theologian.

Vande Kemp shows what the disciplines of psychology and theology can contribute holistically to a collaborative effort from their respective anthropologies. Gold and Mansager understand spirituality holistically, and as a focal point for both disciplines, whereas Ellis offers a non-religious humanist, wholistic perspective which takes no account of the transcendent. Noda, by introducing an Oriental perspective allows for the possibility of understanding the person wholistically and avoiding the dichotomy that remains in Western intellectual thinking. Cheston understands Adlerian thinking as opening the way to holistic development of the person that goes beyond Adler's original thinking. relates scripture to Individual Psychology and introduces the holistic notion of revelation that is not in Adler's original thinking. Slavik understands the person, not as a classical ideal concept, but as a dynamic unit formed holistically within a social field. The abiding aspect of the person, he understands, is a wholistic consciousness.

Critical collaboration exists when psychologists and theologians study original thinkers reciprocally. Disciplines change (hence the possibility of collaboration) but the individual (principle of human and divine life) abides.

REFERENCES

Brinton, D. 1876. *The religious sentiment: Its source and aim.* New York: Henry Holt.

Cheston, S. 2000. Spirituality of encouragement. *Journal of Individual Psychology* 56: 296-304.

Dulles, A. 1969. *Revelation and theology: A history.* New York: Herder & Herder.

Ellis, A. 2000. Spiritual goals and spirited values in psychotherapy. *The Journal of Individual Psychology* 56: 277-84.

Frost, W. 1997. Brian Goodwin's wholism: How holistic is it? *Explorations: Journal for Adventurous Thought* 16: 68-9.

Gold, L. and E. Mansager. 2000. Spirituality: Life task or life process? *Journal of Individual Psychology* 56: 266-76

Mansager, E. 2001. Adlerian psychology and spirituality in critical collaboration. In *Year Book 2001.* London: Adlerian Society of the United Kingdom.

McCool, G. 1977. *Catholic theology in the nineteenth century: The quest for a unity of method.* New York: Seabury.

Noda, S. 2000. The concept of holism in Individual Psychology and Buddhism. *The Journal of Individual Psychology* 56: 285-95.

Ross, E. 1912. *Social psychology: An outline and source book.* New York: Macmillan.

Runes, D. 1963. *Dictionary of philosophy: Ancient, medieval, modern.* New Jersey: Littlefield, Adams.

Slavik, S. 2000. The subject matter of individual psychology. *The Canadian Journal of Adlerian Psychology* 30: 34-44.

Smuts, J. 1927. *Holism and evolution.* London: Macmillan.

—, 1928. Foreword. In *A Catholic view of holism*, by Msgr. Kolbe, New York: Macmillan.

Tyrrell, G. *A much-abused letter.* London: Longmans, Green.

—, 1963/1909. *Christianity and the cross-roads.* London: George Allen & Unwin.

Vande Kemp, H. 2000. Wholeness, holiness, and the care of souls: The Adler-Jahn debate in historical perspective. *The Journal of Individual Psychology* 56: 242-256.

Watts, R. 2000. Biblically based Christian spirituality and Adlerian psychotherapy. *The Journal of Individual Psychology* 56: 316-328.

Weaver, M. 1981. *Letters from a Modernist: The letters of George Tyrrell to Wilfred Ward 1893-1908.* London: Sheed & Ward.

Wenfeng, M. and S. Shaojie. 1991. Classical intuitive thinking in China. *Social Sciences in China* 12: 142-164.

§   §   §

Close Encounters of the Theological Kind

The notions of "holism" and "wholism" may be examined from the points of view of Individual Psychology and theology. The development of our understanding of these notions requires refinement through psychological and theological insights. This brief article is such an attempt. The discipline of psychology makes a contribution from an existential perspective, whereas theology contributes from a transcendental perspective. When psychologists, concerned with the psyche, collaborate with theologians, concerned with the *pneuma*, close encounters of the theological kind occur.

On an earlier occasion I had the opportunity to debate the relationship between Adlerian psychology and theological understanding with a Lutheran minister who is a licensed clinical counsellor (Gregerson & Nelson 1998 & Letters 1999). That exchange led to a degree of wholesome academic refinement as Gregerson notes (Letters 1999, 100). Later, I wrote about *Wholism or Holism in Individual Psychology* (Savage 2001) and critiqued articles written by Vande Kemp, Gold & Mansager, Ellis, Noda, Cheston, Watts and Slavik. In this critique I read Adler as an existentialist philosopher and not as a clinical psychologist. Of these authors, Mansager and Slavik have reacted with varying intensity to the article in which I articulated my understanding of the relationship between Adlerian psychology and theology. Some of their reactions are justifiable while other reactions miss the mark, I believe. I address the ones that miss the mark in an effort to refine the understanding of the relationship between Individual Psychology and theology.

Mansager believes that I have muddied the issue of critical collaboration more than clarified it. He must conclude this, I believe, because he is using an analytical approach: the psychology of religion. That is not the approach in my theological understanding. A psychology of religion is not tantamount to a theological understanding. Nor can the psychology of religion enter that realm of bodily experience and recognize that which is transcendent and in some way "other" than the individual. The psychology of religion recognizes a metaphysics, but that metaphysics need not be transcendent. Von Hügel's (1912) understanding is insightful here. In a word, through the discipline of theology one is able to enter a mystery, a spiritual encounter, whereas through the discipline of the psychology of religion one engages a phenomenon. The latter deals predominately with problems of religion and the former predominately with the mystery of religion. Randall (2001, 74) notes, after acknowledging a debt to Albert Camus and Gabriel Marcel, that "while we *solve* problems we *encounter* mysteries, we *struggle with* absurdities" [author's emphasis]. Entering a mystery requires a theological form of understanding. The theological enterprise does not lend itself satisfactorily to a clinical analytical approach. To theologize is to enter into the spiritual (pneumatic, not psychical) experience of another individual. It is to understand the pneumatological of human experience as comprising the human mystery. It is in entering this realm of experience that one comes to understand and appreciate the distinction between the notions of "holism" and "wholism" with respect to psychology and theology.

Mansager (2001, 69) has it correct when he writes:

From the very outset, [Savage] encourages psychologists and theologians to distinguish between the terms holism and wholism -- establishing the impossibility of the discussion being handled anywhere but in print -- since the words are indistinguishable in pronunciation.

Because the words are indistinguishable in pronunciation the discussion is best handled in print until the notions have become recognized experientially. Words are printed symbols of notions arising from personal experience. I accept written expressions (words) as the "map" of the "territory" to employ Slavik's (2001) terminology. In theology, they symbolize, not describe experience or existence. This descriptive understanding, a psychology of religion, may account for Corsini's lack of differentiation between the notions of wholism and holism.

Slavik's observation, that I have confused the map with the territory in my article, is accurate. This has resulted from a return to descriptive thinking on my part and yielding to the temptation of conceptualizing experience objectively (theoretically). Not to confuse the map with the territory requires a non-analytical way or a phenomenological way of understanding one's experience. Notional or intentional, not conceptual, ways of thinking arise out of phenomenological understanding. Adler's helpful insight was to recognize this notional, not conceptual way of thinking about individual experience as Slavik notes. Adler is easily understood as an existential philosopher from this point of view.

With regard to Smuts's statements, Mansager truly believes that I have misunderstood and misrepresented them. Perhaps. My remarks concern Smuts's intentional understanding, or meaning, not any theoretical concepts framed within his statements. The analytical perspective of the psychology of religion, adopted by Mansager recognizes a theoretical manner of interpretation. My intention is not to re-present or demonstrate, through an analytical or theoretical approach, what Smuts believed or thought. Mansager thinks it is. Rather, I recognize notions that arise from Smuts's understanding. His non-analytical vocabulary describes in terms of notional being that which I have come to understand as Deity, that is, as mystery.

Understanding Deity is not to be equated with an interpretation of Deism. Interpretation of Deism is a speculative activity. It is that speculative activity that Smuts correctly rejects when he concludes "from the facts of Evolution no inference to a [conceptualized] transcendent Mind is justified." It may have helped with understanding the issue were I to have originally written: "Smuts's way of thinking shows how a psychologist's notion of Deity, and not the speculative philosopher's concept of Deism, is more serviceable in understanding religious experience."

Mansager makes reference to Küng to support the statement that psychologists, *qua* psychologists, reject any understanding of Deity or Deism. It is the business of theology, not psychology, he says quoting Küng, to be concerned with whether or not "psychic processes correlate with an altogether transcendental, unconditional, ultimate reality." I wonder. I suggest that psychic processes cannot but correlate with an altogether transcendental reality. Psychology cannot abdicate a relationship with the transcendental. However, it may fail to recognize such a relationship. Existentially, psychology and theology are distinguished but not separable. The "business" of one is the "business" of the other. A phenomenological understanding of religious processes, an encounter with mystery, can lead one to recognize this relationship. An encounter with mystery will disclose that not the "good inviting reasons" of speculative theology (the psychic experience), but the holistic experience of the transcendent other (the pneumatic experience) is what "the believing human names God." The holistic experience, not the wholistic experience, leads the believing human to the notion of Deity. Mansager is correct. "One cannot reason [speculate] to deity by science" any more than one can reason to revelation. In holistic thinking there is no movement of the intellect towards an object that it grasps, but only disclosure of an abiding presence. The Adlerian notion of the goal of religious activity is an example of the dynamic of experience approaching, but not entering, a theological encounter.

Slavik desires to know what I mean by revelation and this may motivate him to continue a discussion that he began earlier in *Explorations.* The fact is that he and I might be closer in our understanding of revelation than is first apparent. "Paradise is here and now and we extract all the messages we can deal with from the world around us," he writes. I agree with the intent of this statement. I would be more content with it were he to have written that "we *intend* all the messages we can deal with." This allows us to recognize further meanings to all the messages we can deal with which arise out of our experience. From an existential perspective revelation is not some content or message in relation to us as "the knower" is in relation to "the known." Rather, revelation is a coming to understand through differentiation, a coming to recognize a mystery. In short, revelation is becoming conscious of a further meaning to what is recognized; it is an understanding beyond the explicit context. Going beyond the explicit context takes one into the realm of theology. Leslie Dewart (1966) has attempted this. In mystery, there is no dichotomy between the knower and the known and the "the Revealer" is "the revealed" and "the Giver" is "the gift." Encountering a mystery extracts no thing but understands notionally through disclosure what is already there – a close encounter of the theological kind.

REFERENCES

Dewart, L. 1966. *The future of belief: Theism in a world come of age.* New York: Herder & Herder.

Gregerson, D. L. and M. D. Nelson. 1998. Striving for righteousness: Perfection as completion. *The Canadian Journal of Adlerian Psychology* 28(2): 21-28.

Letters. (1999). *The Canadian Journal of Adlerian Psychology* 19 (2): 95-101.

Mansager, E. 2001. Holy 'Wholly Holes'! A response to Allan Savage. *The Canadian Journal of Adlerian Psychology* 31(1): 68-77.

Randall, A. 2001. Beyond the barricade: Reflective meditations on religion and the human spirit. *Explorations: Journal for Adventurous Thought* 19: 71-100.

Savage, A. 2001. Wholism or holism in Individual Psychology and theology. *The Canadian Journal of Adlerian Psychology* 31(1): 23-38.

Slavik, S. 2001. If I understand Dr. Savage correctly.... *The Canadian Journal of Adlerian Psychology* 31 (1): 78-80.

Von Hügel, F. 1912. *Eternal life: A study of its implications and applications.* Edinburgh: T & T Clark.

§   §   §

The Philosophical Context of Adler's Individual Psychology

Existentialism: A philosophical current started in the past century by the Dane, Sören Kierkegaard (+1855), and developed by recent scholars (Heidegger, Jaspers, Marcel, Abbagnano) in a variety of interpretations and connotations....For Kierkegaard (a Protestant) the tragic discovery of this real existence resolves itself in an appeal to the supernatural and, what is more, to an appeal without further ado to Christianity; but the other existentialists have eliminated this religious motive in order to stand aside in the *problematicity* of life and thought, and be free from the worries of definitive solutions (Emphasis in original). [1]

Since Individual Psychology is not interested in the verbal expression of feelings, but only in the intensity of the movement by which they are expressed, it will evaluate the members of various religions not by the way they represent their feelings, but by the movement of the whole individual follower, i.e. by their fruits. That these fruits must be recognised *sub specie aeternitatis* (in the light of eternity) may be said parentetically. Individual Psychology does not deny that the religions with their powers, their church institutions, their influence on school and education, have a strong advantage. It will be satisfied in the practical application of its science to protect and further the sacred good of brotherly love where the religions have lost their influence (Alfred Adler, 1933). [2]

Introduction

This essay intends to illustrate three points. First, this article intends to show that Adler was a product of one of the philosophical systems of the time, i.e., German existentialism. Secondly, it will be shown that contemporary phenomenological philosophy throws light on Adler's Individual Psychology. This makes his work universally applicable. Thirdly, the religious roots of existentialism are a strength, not a liability, in understanding the human condition and ought not to be forgotten by Adlerian psychologists. Slavik (1997), an Adlerian thinker, recognizes the existential aspect of Adler's thinking as "contextual philosophy" composed of the events that constitute an individual's experience of life.

Phenomenological Perspective

Jellema (1963, 81) observes a change from classical thinking to phenomenological thinking and writes:

we in the mid-twentieth century are witnessing a change similar in import to the change around 1650; namely, the emergence of a new "mind," radically different in approach from the "modern mind," and already viewing the "obvious" notion of Reality previously held as something antiquated and alien.

I suggest that Adler and his Individual Psychology is an example of this new radically different mind that attempts to understand experience without the assistance of previously held notions. In short, Adler is a phenomenological thinker. Lowe (1982, 165) notes: "We are so accustomed to philosophizing from an extrinsic standpoint, whether Cartesian or Platonic, that we can no longer comprehend the phenomenological standpoint within the world." We need to de-familiarize ourselves with Cartesian and Platonic thought forms and familiarize ourselves with a phenomenological approach. Adler's Individual Psychology does this.

In classical thinking, theoretical questions and answers are governed by a fixed idea of nature. That is, what is rational has been idealized (reified) in order to be comprehended by reason. The notion of contingency being anything but accidental was impossible to conceive (Torrance 1969, 61). Moreover, truth expressed in theoretical terms has become fixed in a particular form of expression that itself was perceived to be as valid as the truth. Researchers, not aware of this aberration in which the means have become idealized ends (idealistic goals), make interpretive mistakes. Adler's Individual Psychology presents a philosophical option. Adler's "non-fixity" in understanding helps us avoid the interpretive mistakes of the idealistic philosophers. His is an phenomenological interpretation. In phenomenological interpretation, existence is understood as becoming, unity is understood as relational and necessity is replaced by option. These notions are easily recognizable in Adler's Individual Psychology.

As western culture continues to evolve, traditional conceptualization becomes increasingly less helpful. Skolimowski (1973, 105), after an exposé of the limitations of conventional descriptions, offers his understanding of a new knowledge. It is phenomenological knowledge.

> Thus, new knowledge based on different kinds of descriptions is not only an epistemological imperative, it is also a social imperative: it is an imperative for our survival. What we are seeking, without perhaps being fully aware of it, is not so much improved science, or more science, but a different idiom for living, a different idiom for our interaction with nature and cosmos. We must liberate ourselves from the pernicious assumption that present Western rationality and present Western science are the alpha and omega of all knowledge.

Phenomenological thinking, which is existential understanding about human experience, continues to develop. The Middle Ages embodied an ecclesiastical culture that embraced all strata of European society. Science, philosophy and theology were experienced as one *summa*. However, during the Renaissance, science and technology, and to some degree philosophy, began to develop autonomously and free from the tutelage of the church. Modern thinking developed independently and, in many cases, in opposition to classical philosophy and theology (Kroner 1951, 74). Philosophical development is continually taking place, and the western hermeneutic is seeking to end its "cultural provincialism" and to provide a new threshold of interpretation (Tracy 1988, 56). In short we cannot live with fossilized thresholds. Adler's Individual Psychology assists in ending this "cultural provincialism."

Theoretical scientific understanding originated with the philosophers who were prior to Plato and Aristotle and prepared the way for a phenomenological interpretation. Murray (1940, 36) writes:

> The early philosophers of the sixth and fifth centuries B.C. were more like men of science with a strong taste for generalization. Their problems were concerned with the physical world: they made researches in geometry, geography, medicine, astronomy, natural history and were apt to sum up their conclusions in sweeping apophthegms...Socrates, the father of the Attic school of philosophy, turning away from natural science with its crude generalizations, concentrated his attention on man, and particulary on the analysis of ordinary speech and current ideas.

Adler also "concentrated his attention on man" in his Individual Psychology, by way of phenomenological thinking. Adler constructs eidetic objects that have no extra-mental existence, ideal or otherwise (Ryba 1991, 182). These fictions, or eidetic notions, cause movement in an individual which is capable of study through Adler's Individual Psychology.

Traditional western analytical interpretation maintains that there must be some cause existing independently behind all effects. It follows that were the cause to be known, the effects would be predictable. Discussing modern developments in the cognitive sciences, Searle (1984, 45) points out an assumption within rationalist thinking which many find no longer tests as true. This assumption "goes as far back as Leibnitz and probably as far as Plato. It is the assumption that a mental achievement must have theoretical causes." Murray (1940, 40) also notes that the assumption of theoretical causes begins with Plato. However, this is not so in Adler's Individual Psychology. He makes no assumptions according to the classical mode. Rather than assuming, Adler's phenomenological interpretation suggests a direction in which development may occur.

Since Adler's thinking is not determined by pre-existing theoretical causes, it presents as a new threshold of understanding. In Individual Psychology, as a phenomenological methodology, there is no past or future that concretely exists; there is only the perpetual present moment of existence which is susceptible to interpretation. In practice, past events (i.e., memories) are recalled to the present moment, and hypothetical conceptions of the future (i.e., models) are yet to be actualized. In Husserl's (1970, 160) words: "Perception is related only to the *present*. But this present is always meant as having an endless *past* behind it and an open *future* before it" [Husserl's italics].

Phenomenological methods disclose new thresholds of ordered understanding without prejudice to scholastic understanding. Phenomenological inquiry need not be sharply divorced from traditional speculative methodology. An integrative approach is possible. The present moment (movement) is not divorced from the past but rather has evolved from it (Sokolowski 1974, 167). Bloom (1987, 42) cites the evolutionary development of Decartes's thought:

> Descartes had a whole wonderful world of old beliefs, of prescientific experience and articulations of the order of things, beliefs firmly and evenly fanatically held, *before* [italics mine] he even began his systematic and radical doubt.

As well, Bloom (1987, 310) notes that Heidegger returned to pre-existing thought forms in developing his ideas.

> But it was Heidegger, practically alone, for whom the study of Greek philosophy became truly central, a pressing concern for his meditation on being....A new beginning was imperative, and he turned with open mind to the ancients. But he did not focus on Plato or Aristotle....Heidegger was drawn instead to the pre-Socratic philosophers, from whom he hoped to discover another understanding of being to help him replace the exhausted one inherited from Plato and Aristotle, which he and Nietzsche thought to be at the root of both Christianity and modern science.

According to Ferguson (1992, 122) Stephen Hawking presents a similar position in his thinking.

> [Stephen Hawking] doesn't hesitate to admit that an earlier conclusion was incorrect or incomplete. That's the way his science 'and perhaps all good science' advances, and one of the reasons why physics seems so full of paradoxes.

Finally, Dewart (1989, 31) notes a similar evolutionary development occurring in epistemological thinking. He writes: "The phenomenological method...is not the diametric opposite of the ontological; it is a more comprehensive one than the latter, whose merits it preserves and whose inadequacies it tries to remedy." Adler's Individual psychology recognizes certain phenomenological thresholds of interpretation.

WORKS CONSULTED

Bloom, A. 1987. *The closing of the American mind: How higher education has failed democracy and impoverished the souls of today's students.* New York: Simon & Schuster.

Brunner, E. 1942. *Man in revolt: A Christian anthropology.* London: Lutterworth.

Dalkey, N. C. 1972. The Delphi Method: An Experimental Study of Group Opinion. In *Studies in the quality of life: Delphi and decision making,* edited by N.C. Dalkey, 13-55. Lexington, Massachusetts: Lexington.

Darroch, V. and R. Silvers. 1982. *Interpretive human studies: An introduction to phenomenological research.* (Ontario Institute for Studies in Education). Washington: University Press of America.

Dewart, L. 1989. *Evolution and consciousness: The role of speech in the origin and development of human nature.* Toronto: University of Toronto Press.

Ferguson, K. 1992. *Stephen Hawking: Quest for a theory of everything.* New York: Bantam.

Fontinell, E. 1967. The Need for Radicalism. In *The future of belief debate,* edited by G. Baum, 109-14. New York: Herder & Herder.

Hodges, H. A. 1979. *God beyond knowledge.* London: Macmillan.

Husserl, E. 1970. *The crisis of European sciences and transcendental phenomenology.* Evanston, Illinois: Northwestern University Press.

Ihde, D. 1977. *Experimental phenomenology: An introduction.* New York: G P Putnam's Sons.

Jellema, D. 1963. Toward investigating the 'post-modern mind': A working paper. *Journal for the Scientific Study of Religion* 3: 81-5.

Keen, E. 1970. *Three faces of being: Toward an existential clinical psychology.* New York: Appleton-Century-Crofts.

Kroner, R. 1951. *Culture and faith.* Chicago: University of Chicago Press.

Lowe, D. M. 1982. *History of bourgeois perception.* Chicago: University of Chicago Press.

Madison, G. B. 1988. *The hermeneutics of postmodernity: Figures and themes.* Bloomington: Indiana University Press.

Murray, G. 1940. *Stoic, Christian and humanist.* London: C. A. Watts.

Peters, K. E. 1971. The concept of God and the method of science: An exploration of the possibility of scientific theology. PhD thesis, Columbia University, New York.

Ryba, T. 1991. *The essence of phenomenology and its meaning for the scientific study of religion.* New York: Peter Lang.

Searle, J. 1984. *Minds, brains and science.* London: Penguin.

Slavik, S. 1997. Individual psychology as contextual philosophy. *The Canadian Journal of Individual Psychology* 27 (1): 85-98.

Skolimowski, H. 1973. The Twilight of Physical Descriptions and the Ascent of Normative Models. In *The world system: Models, norms, applications,* edited by E. Laszlo, 99-118. New York: George Braziller.

Sokolowski, R. 1974. *Husserlian Meditations: How words present things.* Evanston, Illinois: Northwestern University Press.

Streng, F. 1991. Purposes and investigative principles in the phenomenology of religion: A reconstruction. *Journal for the Study of Religion* 4: 3-17.

Tarnas, R. 1991. *The passion of the western mind: Understanding ideas that have shaped our world view.* New York: Ballantine.

Torrance, T. 1969. *Theological science.* London: Oxford University Press.

Tracy, D. 1988. Theology and the Hermeneutical Turn. In *Hermeneutics and the tradition,* edited by D. O. Dahlstrom, 46-57. Washington: American Catholic Philosophical Association. (Proceedings of the American Catholic Philosophical Association 50.)

Von Bertalanffy, L. 1968. *General system theory: Foundations, development, applications.* New York: George Braziller.

Watts, F. and M. Williams. 1988. *The psychology of religious knowing.* Cambridge: Cambridge University Press.

Westphal, M. 1984. *God, guilt, and death: An existential phenomenology of religion.* Bloomington, Indiana: Indiana University Press.

Young, R. 1988. *Psychotherapy: Acceptance or denial.* Ilminster, Somerset, U.K.: Somerset Independent University Press.

CHAPTER 8

PHENOMENOLOGICAL THRESHOLDS OF THEOLOGICAL INQUIRY

ABSTRACT

The task of theology is to identify trends in the thinking of the faithful with respect to our understanding of God's involvement in human activity in the world. Heidegger and Husserl attempted to develop ways of understanding that were more adequate in explaining human experience than traditional metaphysics. In his attempts, Heidegger, rejects criticism that his approach is atheistic (Robinson & Cobb 1963, 35). Phenomenological theology inquires into the meaning given to a religious presence in the world. It does not merely describe a religious presence. I would argue that this is a poetic purpose. There is some institutional tardiness in accommodating the new threshold of phenomenological and theological thought. To some degree western churches are still being influenced by traditional concepts. As a methodology, phenomenological understanding is capable of transcending cultures, since it is not bound to the ideal categories of specific cultures. Theologians of the Modernist movement sought to express theological truths in modern images and terms. They introduced new thresholds of interpretation, i.e., phenomenological understanding.

Scholastic philosophy is limited in its ability to interpret contemporary experience. Modernism, as a hermeneutical movement, prefigured and provided the context for a phenomenological interpretation of a poetic kind. Phenomenological theology is essentially different from theoretical theology in that phenomenological theology understands the eidetic objects of consciousness, whereas theoretical theology interprets the objects of classical idealism. Poets are phenomenological thinkers whose ways of thinking are making personal and novel contributions to theological understanding. Poets create new thresholds of interpretation. First Threshold: Interpretation of ideals becomes participatory understanding. Second Threshold: Knowledge of ideals becomes participatory knowledge. Third threshold: Idealistic language and interpretation become participatory language and understanding. Introduction. Notions derived from the thinking of the later Heidegger (Robinson & Cobb 1963: ix) and the thought of Husserl provide the matter and framework for this essay. Admittedly, employing German thoughts in an English idiom presents its difficulties (ix). Yet, the task of theology is to identify trends in the thinking of the faithful with respect to our understanding of God's activity in the world even when those trends take us away from traditional understanding "by upholding relational approaches to truth and reality rather different from those prevalent in mainstream Western culture" (Endean 2000, 54). Human reflection, engaged at the threshold of phenomenology and theology, reveals that "the thinker speaks being. The poet names the Holy" (Robinson & Cobb 1963, 45). This presents us with a completely new situation requiring a relational (phenomenological) interpretation of experience.

1. Phenomenological inquiry

Phenomenological thinking concerns itself with both being and with metaphysics which has elsewhere been described as the 'Queen of the Sciences' (Gilson 1968). Streng (1991, 4) notes that phenomenological theology has tried "to avoid any procedures for understanding that derive from 'positivist' or 'rationalist' presuppositions, on the grounds that [it does] not allow the *religious* meaning of the data to become known" [Streng's italics]. As a kind of poetic naming of the holy, phenomenological understanding is not rooted in the "angst" of existentialism. Rather, it is rooted in the "calmness and ineffability which replaces 'angst'" (Robinson & Cobb 1963, 139). Concerning the purpose of a phenomenological understanding, Laycock (1986, 5) writes that phenomenological theology:

> seeks to discover its Subject Matter, the Divine (*theos*), in that web of intuitively articulable necessities in which phenomena are caught and seeks to do so by means of the reductive-eidetic-reconstructive techniques characteristic of phenomenology. Phenomenological theology, in Husserl's exquisite phrase, seeks to reach "God without God" [Laycock's italics].

According to Brunner (1942, 46) phenomenological theology makes inquiries into the pre-reflective human understanding and that "all that the poets and artists tell us about man usually comes from this source," that is, a source of pre-reflective human understanding. The type of theological understanding crafted by the phenomenological method of interpretation derives from an existential, not idealistic, attitude to life. Möeller (1968, 424) distinguishes between the terms "existential" and "existentialist." He writes:

The primary cultural datum with which to begin reflection on Christian anthropology is that of the *existential approach* [Möeller's emphasis]. We do not say "existentialist," for this term denotes a region of philosophical systematization, whereas what we are here concerned with is a global approach to reality.

In short, he claims that "existentialist" reduces the existential approach to an ideal of traditional metaphysics. He suggests that the phenomenological approach ought to replace the classical philosophical theory of ideals. Jordaan and Jordaan (1989, 822) and King (1968, 378) cite Søren Kierkegaard's work as an example of existential inquiry. Brunner (1942, 546) explains that

it was as a Christian philosopher that Kierkegaard created the "Existential" philosophy, it was as a Christian thinker that Ebner discovered the theme of "I-Thou" . No Greek, however great a genius, would have ever understood such a theme. It was as a Biblical thinker that Martin Buber recognized the significance of the contrasts between "I" and "It," "I" and "Thou."

Kierkegaard, initiated a kind of poetic inquiry into life which other philosophers have followed upon. The so-called Modernist movement discloses this kind of poetic inquiry in the thinking of George Tyrrell.

2. Phenomenological Thresholds Arising From the So-called Modernist Movement

Modernist thought developed from the theological hermeneutic introduced about 1900 in Europe and England that viewed tradition and dogma as symbolic expressions of religious experience. It has existential/phenomenological roots. Liderbach (2001, 26) tells us that "Modernists insisted upon the importance of phenomena as the starting point of a description of an occurrence." Poets insist on the same. Edwards (1977:395), in an entry in the *Fontana Dictionary of Modern Thought* writes that within the Anglican tradition the Modernist theologians were known as 'modern churchmen,' and the most influential were perhaps H D A Major and W R Inge. About a generation later Modernism made its appearance in the United States.

Within the Roman Catholic tradition, Dulles (1992, 18) observes that Modernism "permeates much of the existential phenomenology and theological empiricism that became popular since Vatican II." Loisy (1857-1940) and Tyrrell (1861-1909) were significant representatives of Modernism and their work consisted of evaluating the symbolic expressions of religious interpretation of their day. These men "were not organisers of reform movements; they were writers and scholars absorbed in their work," according to Kurtz (1986, 109). As traditional and classical religious images are foreign to contemporary culture, so the terms of the Modernist movement have lost their significance due to a change in the contemporary social and cultural context. *Sacramentum Mundi* notes that with the "passing of the original situation, the philosophy of existence has lost its predominant role" and becomes "a philosophy of 'participation'– in other words, a new metaphysics."

Poetry, like classical philosophy, also fails when its criteria are no longer satisfied by well-chosen symbols. Garbett (1947, 272) writes: "Large numbers regard the claims of Christianity as inconsistent with modern ways of thought. Phrases like the 'Fatherhood of God,' 'Salvation through Christ' and 'Life after death' seem to them meaningless platitudes." New understandings need to be constructed.

Maurer (1967, 24) suggests that Leslie Dewart's efforts at dehellenisation (a Modernist endeavour) is "intended to prepare the way for the future of belief in which it will take on the new cultural form of existential phenomenology." Theological dehellenisation is an example of the phenomenological method of interpretation replacing the classical method of interpretation. Dehellenization presents a new threshold of activity for phenomenology and theology. Lowe (1982, 165) observes: "We are so accustomed to philosophizing from an extrinsic standpoint, whether Cartesian or Platonic, that we can no longer comprehend the phenomenological standpoint within the world." Nipkow (1993, 60) notes that, even though not clearly defined, phenomenological understanding is clearly underway in Catholic and Protestant traditions:

> In the Catholic domain, the striving towards a liberation of practical theology from dogmatical tutelage and the turning away from a practical theology as "applied theology" is relatively recent....Protestantism can draw on a longer tradition of the historical application of the social and cultural "*Lebenswelt.*"

This *Lebenswelt*, discounted as merely subjective and ignored by the dominant traditions of Western philosophy "is desperately in need of disciplined exploration and clarification" says Wild (1964, 13). As a result of this discounted view by Western philosophy many of us miss the opportunity to see a new threshold of theological inquiry that the Modernist movement has presented through the dehellenization of theology.

An eidetic object is a phenomenological construct. In classical thinking, theoretical theological questions and answers are governed by a fixed idea of nature. The notion of contingency being anything but accidental was impossible to conceive by classical philosophy (Torrance 1969, 61). Moreover, truth expressed in theoretical terms became fixed in a particular form of expression that itself was perceived to be as valid as the truth. Researchers, not aware of this aberration in which the means becomes equivalent to the ends, make interpretive mistakes. Thus, for such researchers Seidel believes that their data become reified. "Then [we] base our understandings of the phenomena on these reified objects and, in the process, lose the phenomena," he says (Seidel 1991, 114). Fixity of expression is not a problem in phenomenological understanding; since concepts have no independent existence there is no necessity to become fixed. This "fixed expression" of truth remains a problem for scholastic theologians. However, it is not confined to them. Ferguson (1992, 17) records this same problematic of fixed expression developing in the scientific disciplines. Keen (1970, 352), also, cites this problem occurring in psychology. The new threshold of understanding in phenomenological theology is that a relational and dynamic conception of truth replaces a fixed idea of truth.

Although phenomenological thought is distinct from classical thought it has not developed *sui generis* (out of itself). Dondeyne notes that philosophical schools of thought are related and do not come into being independently of each other. Dondeyne (1963, 132) writes about St. Thomas' viewpoint:

> But let us not forget that this way of looking at man and his links with the world is the legacy of medieval humanism, which was born from the union of Greco-Roman thought with Christian theism and personalism.

In phenomenological appreciation, existence is understood as becoming, unity is understood as relational and necessity is replaced by option. All these notions have their roots in theological Modernism. But, as well, these roots are characteristic of poetry. From a phenomenological perspective, existence can be philosophically or poetically interpreted. Since phenomenological theology is a kind of poetry, (a pre-reflective view), I consider below some poetic phenomenological thresholds of theological inquiry.

3. Poetic thresholds of phenomenological theology

Theologians are continually searching for new and meaningful ways to interpret religious experience (Garbett 1947, 24; Bent 1969, 6). Some draw on the new language of a phenomenological theology as a kind of poetry. I agree with Morreall that there are no hidden meanings to be disclosed in phenomenological theological language. Morreall (1983:56) writes:

> My conclusions regarding various appeals to hidden meaning for theological language, then, are negative....Our words are based on our intentions, and so if theological language is possible then theological intentions must be possible....We should not spend our time trying to appeal to hidden meanings for theological language.

Rather than disclose hidden meanings, as in an allegorical approach, phenomenological theological enquiry attributes religious meaning to phenomena, thus freeing understanding from allegorical limitations (Capps 1984, 17). Poetic understanding is similar to phenomenological understanding. Both originate in experience. Poetry is original. As well, phenomenological theology is original theology, according to Laycock (1986, 2). That the phenomenological method presents a new threshold for theological enquiry can be demonstrated to philosophers and theologians "but whether phenomenologists of religion have accurately grasped what is demanded by these methods is dubitable" (Ryba 1991, 231).

Unlike poetry, classical theology is "a deductive science that uses propositions of revelation as premises" (Dulles 1992, 17). This deductive type of science appeals to the western mind and has made classical terms of reference and understanding normative. Medieval clerics interpreted experience within theoretical formulae. Poetical interpretation frees the interpreter from the idealism of classical theology. However, there is a remnant of thinkers who chose to think classically. Of this remnant, Seasoltz (1983, 57) writes: "They can live with twentieth-century physics, sociology, economics, and technology, but they want sixteenth or seventeenth-century religion." To this day much theological thinking appears as sixteenth or seventeenth-century religious artifact which has been preserved by the classical threshold of meaning.

Maxwell (1986, 17) suggests phenomenological interpretation is an attempt "to get inside the mind of the believer," a goal which poets may, in fact, achieve. In contemporary culture, poetic understanding presents a counterbalance to scholastic understanding. Poetic interpretations do not conform to the reasoned order of deductive science. In Mallard's (1977,

34) words "poetry...is just that formal mode of language which recalls *presence*" which "is in turn the quality of the real." Jesus, Paul of Tarsus, Augustine, and Francis of Assisi, according to Mallard (1977, 8), are poets in this sense. The poetic understanding of religious experience is, in fact, of a similar kind to a philosophical phenomenological understanding that discloses a new awareness of the relationships within experience.

Koestenbaum (1967, 175) reminds us that phenomenological theological inquiry incorporates insights from both rational and poetic thought. In poetic understanding each person engages in imaginative thinking and Mallard (1977, 8) writes of Jesus that he "taught in parables;" of Paul that life was interpreted by him "through a cluster of images, metaphors, and symbols;" of Francis that he possessed a "child-like vision." As well, he notes of Augustine that "certainly no one accuses Augustine of Hippo, despite his neoplatonist and dialectic refinements, of being closed to sensuous, poetic language." In constructing liturgical texts, Puthanangady (1990, 337) notes that "it is very important that the descriptive and poetic style be followed because these texts appeal primarily to emotions." Poetry expresses emotions more deeply than prose.

Phenomenological interpretation is not uniformly presented. Various phenomenological perspectives introduce new thresholds to western theology. These various perspectives are rooted in an existential understanding. "The great figures of the nineteenth century, men such as Schleiermacher, Ritschl and Newman, have powerfully shaped our contemporary problematic [of God]," writes Macquarrie (1975, 87). Since these authors have helped to introduce a phenomenological way of thinking into modern theology they are pioneers in providing alternative interpretations to the dominant classical interpretive perspective of the West. The classical perspective is "decreasingly viable or useful" since contemporary western culture is no longer Hellenist (Robinson 1967, 80).

Within contemporary thinking, a potential renaissance is in the making as the phenomenological method reveals new thresholds of understanding within western culture. Ryba (1991, xiv) notes that "many observers both inside and outside the Roman Catholic Church make the inference that its theology may be on the verge of another grand synthesis...which might...supplant Thomism." This grand synthesis would be contingent upon the abandonment of traditional theoretical thinking (Tymieniecka 1962, xiv). Dermot Lane notes that pluralism in theology has always been present in the church to some degree. This pluralism is "more evident today in view of the absence of a universally acceptable philosophy" (Lane 1989, 72). Hinners (1967, 208) notes that the "current method of integrating and developing our Greek conceptual heritage has failed to project a future of belief which is even adequate for the present." There is evidence to suggest that in formal investigative theology and popular devotional theology, traditional interpretations are changing (Dillenberger 1969, 28; Lonergan 1969, 172). Religious institutions and customs are no longer perceived as given from "on high," as once was the case. Historical, geographical and human agencies all play a role in shaping the cultural, social and intellectual environment of the life-world. Also, the number of theologians accepting that there is no "someone" external to experience determining affairs in this life is increasing. The contemporary perception is that many factors are at work in conjunction with our own efforts. The way forward, I suggest, may be in a series of thresholds of poetical phenomenological understanding for theological inquiry.

4. First Threshold: Interpretation of ideals shifts to participatory understanding

Waardenburg (1973, 117) writes: "The 'new style' phenomenological research in religion interprets 'meaning'...in terms of connections existing between concrete people and those data which have a religious significance for them." In phenomenological theology one must inquire into a multitude of concepts, subjectively formed, that are extremely diverse in their meaning "so that the questions of agreement, disagreement, and truth can be formulated" (Neville 1991, 9). Phenomenological inquiry is influencing Anglican and Roman Catholic theological interpretation. Shea's (1980, 18) observation concerning phenomenological inquiry is significant:

> The thrust in [phenomenological] understanding that may be new for Catholics is that dogmas are an extremely important moment of the faith and the theologizing process but they are not the only moment.

Heinrich Ott (1967, 134), from the perspective of ecumenical inquiry into the disclosure of the meaning of spiritual values, writes:

> Again, although the Roman Catholic Church cannot alter the dogmas which it has defined in virtue of its teaching office, yet it in no way knows what future formulations will appear as a result of the process of understanding and interpretation. That someday a future pope will authoritatively interpret or reformulate one or another of the doctrinal teachings that have divided the churches, e.g., the doctrine of papal infallibility, in such a way that it could be acceptable to us Protestants, upon that rests a genuine ecumenical hope.

It is highly probable that for doctrinal teaching to be reformulated, a Pope would need to abandon the classical interpretation in favour of a phenomenological understanding. Pope John Paul II (1994, 35) seems to approve phenomenological inquiry within contemporary thought when he writes:

> In gaining some distance from positivistic convictions, contemporary thought has made notable advances toward the ever more complete discovery of man, recognizing among other things the value of metaphorical and symbolic language. Contemporary hermeneutics, examples of which are found in the work of Paul Ricoeur or, from a different perspective, in the work of Emmanuel Lévinas – presents the truth about man and the world from new angles.

That God is not responsible for everything anymore introduces a new threshold for inquiry in western theological thought. A co-responsibile and co-creative relationship is disclosed in a phenomenological understanding of the life-world. This is a significant disclosure because persons now identify themselves as co-responsible agents in a relationship and as being co-creators of their life-world. In a classical approach this understanding of co-creatorship is not tenable. In phenomenological approach it is. Merleau-Ponty (1964, 75) offers this criticism of the classical approach:

> The Catholic critics wish for things to reveal a God-directed orientation of the world and wish for man 'like things' to be nothing but a nature heading toward its perfection.

Theologians continue to look for new interpretations in seeking answers to their questions and consciously advance beyond this classical position. Theological interpretation is undergoing an *aggiornamento* and becoming disengaged from a culture that no longer exists as it enters new thresholds of interpretation. It is generally understood, particularly among Roman Catholics, that *aggiornamento* began with Pope John XXIII. However, as Hurley (1969, 68) says:

> It is no belittlement of Pope John to suggest that he was not the creator of this renewal movement, which already existed before his pontificate; that what he did was to welcome and give its name *(aggiornamento)* and aim to the whole movement, to extend to it the full sympathy and encouragement of his person and of his office and to emphasize its implications for Christian unity.

To be effective, *aggiornamento* requires a new, distinct threshold to replace the classical one. This replacement involves understanding individual persons phenomenologically as participants, co-creators within and of their *Lebenswelt*. It is of interest that Tillich (1965, 184) does not seem to limit this co-creativity to human beings but, by a different term, attributes it to non-human beings:

> I mean that, despite human weaknesses, there is something in man that God did not want to destroy....God took a risk, and we must take a risk. He took a risk in permitting man to reach his full humanity....I use the word spontaneity here for animals and plants, and probably even molecules....but I cannot describe this process fully. I learned the fact from biologists and neurologists.

The co-participation in divine creativity by all creatures is the "risk" God took, which "anticipates" possible failure. Steyn (1994, 285) identifies the understanding of "co-creator" relationship as being characteristic of the New Age consciousness.

Relational understanding, is an evolution in methodology, resulting from the development of new thresholds and does not occur simply for novelty's sake, as if contemporary thought were merely tired of classical expression. Rather, phenomenological theological inquiry seeks new meaning out of spiritual necessity. Gilkey (1975, 210) tells us that phenomenological interpretation occurs "with a sense of the holy or sacred as the prior condition for the meaningfulness of *any* form of theology" [Gilkey's italics]. Further, Garbett (1947, 304) remarks: "The Church will not be able to meet the great claims of tomorrow unless in its own life there is holiness." Further, Kaufman (1990, 61) writes: "Theological reconstruction is not undertaken simply to satisfy some mere intellectual or speculative impulse; it is a demand of the life of faith itself." Many contemporary western-educated individuals understand themselves as faithful co-responsible agents and seek new thresholds for theological inquiry that will express their participatory role in the religious interpretation of the life-world. Classical theological understanding does not falsify the task, rather, it is inadequate for the contemporary task.

In western theological understanding, debate has moved from the question of the structure of religious language (an issue of classical interpretation) to "the more radical question of its possibility as a mode of meaningful discourse" (an issue of phenomenological understanding) in which the interpreter is part of the interpretation (Gilkey 1969, 13). That the interpreter is part of the interpretation is a poetic notion. In an article entitled 'Renewal of the Doctrine of Man,' Charles Möeller (1968, 435) writes of personal theological interpretive structures: "it is not by escaping from the real weight of these structures that we will be saved, but through them, by accepting our condition; not by trying to outstrip time but by living the *theologia crucis* or existential threshold."

In phenomenological interpretation the Christian's life-world is the *theologia crucis* in which religious matters must be engaged. The *theologia crucis* is an existential threshold. For most western Christians, modernity is the context of the *theologia crucis*, and "modernity can and will no longer borrow the criteria...from the models supplied by another epoch; *it has to create its normativity out of itself*" [Habermas's italics](Habermas 1992, 7). According to Kaufman (1990, x), in an existential understanding of the *theologia crucis*, theology becomes "fundamentally an activity of *construction* (and reconstruction) not description or exposition, as it has ordinarily been understood in the past" [Kaufman's italics].

This understanding of theological construction is similar to Lonergan's notion of a theological model. Lonergan (1972, xii) writes:

> By a model is not meant something to be copied or imitated. By a model is not meant a description of reality or a hypothesis about reality. It is simply an intelligible, interlocking set of terms and relations that it may be well to have about when it comes to describing reality or to forming hypotheses.

We seek to understand ourselves in a language adapted to the world we experience, and, indeed, "we cannot legitimately and meaningfully conceive except in terms of the world *we* inhabit" [Gilkey's italics] (Gilkey 1975, 102). Yet in theology, there is still no hermeneutic, no clear method, no set of rules to secure a definite interpretation and understanding of religious experience. However, Berger (1980, ix) suggests, "theological thought should follow an inductive approach...that begins with ordinary human experience...and moves on from there to religious affirmations about the nature of reality." This is a relational approach that suggests a kind of poetic activity and phenomenological understanding.

Failing to understand the principle of poetic activity and phenomenological understanding, some early Christian missionaries saw nothing but ignorant superstition in the religious activity of indigenous peoples. According to Graham, the Counter-Reformation in Europe had repercussions in Canada. The thirst to evangelize, to suffer martyrdom, and to found new religious orders was evidence of new enthusiasms for religious life. Further, Graham (1990, 26) writes:

> Though furs and fish accounted for most of the interest, the harvesting of heathen souls was not a negligible concern. The King made that a condition for the fur monopoly; and Samuel de Champlain made it his business to bring those 'living without God and without religion like brute beasts' to a knowledge of Christ. Like Champlain the missionaries did not credit as true religion the beliefs and rituals they found among the Indians. The native

cosmology was 'fable', the native holy men were 'sorcerers', and the native ceremonies were 'superstitions'. Nor did the missionaries appreciate why their own cosmology, holy men, and ceremonies might have struck many shamans as nonsense at best and bad medicine at worst.

But phenomenologically innovative understanding or the shift to new thresholds does not occur without resistance. Waardenburg (1973, 131) notes that there are certain "mechanisms of repression at play within each society with regard to deviant or at least diverging intentions wanting to express themselves, against those intentions which are generally admitted."

5. Second Threshold: Knowledge of ideals shifts to participatory knowledge

This section discusses the philosophical shift in epistemological thinking from a classical to a phenomenological way of thinking. Sontag (1969, 28) states: "For all too long theologians, while realizing their kinship to philosophy, have acted like men determined to think that some particular philosophy was required of them." In theological thinking, characteristics modeled on anthropomorphic understanding are often predicated of that which is divine. Further, these predicates are often understood to be real in the public mind as constituting God *in se* (in himself). That the understanding of the divine is believed to be "other," or is interpreted as "other," does not reveal anything of a divine nature or even whether God, or gods, exist. In contrast to classical thought, phenomenological thought does not present objective divinity and Platt (1989, 106) notes: "Whether there is *in fact* [Platt's italics] a divine component or whether such experiences are simply a projection from human consciousness does not affect the phenomenological description." Classical philosophy posits that a true, absolute being, one who is all-powerful, all-knowing and transcendent, personally exists over and above the temporal world, imparting knowledge to the knower. In classical philosophy absolute being lacks the potential for any development or evolution. This contrasts with phenomenological philosophy in which an evolutionary understanding of "to be" occurs and relationships are constructed rather than theoretical categories recognized. In the West, phenomenological philosophy has been gaining credibility since the beginning of the Reformation.

I follow Sontag in that philosophy, properly understood, supports theology. He (Sontag 1969, 24) suggests: "When philosophy regains its rightful place, asking questions that no science can determine for it, it becomes less certain but also more flexible so that theology can once again utilize its support." Gilson (1968) discusses the relationship between metaphysics and theology in a pithy essay entitled, 'On Behalf of the Handmaid.'

Philosophy, which gives form to doctrine, is a natural human activity and is not to be confused with revelation (Avis 1990, 35; Prentice 1971, 28; Tyrrell 1907, 229). Within this shift, from a static knowledge to a participatory knowledge, subjectivity is not to be confused with subjectivism. Torrance (1969, 81), writing of the subjective in the Christian legacy, states: "This subjective aspect, more evident in the Lutheran than in the Calvinist Reformation, was fostered everywhere by the spirit of the Renaissance in its humanism and individualism." Heelan (1977, 8) offers a phenomenological criticism of objectivism in keeping with the thought of this paper. Subjectivism and objectivism denote a specific doctrine or system of knowledge, whereas subjectivity and objectivity are notions connoting a phenomenological and personal view of the life-world. Stanton (1989, 5) notes what is omitted in a biography may tell as much as what is included. The context in which interpreters interpret ought to be known and understood by the audience avoid mistakes associated with confusing subjectivism and subjectivity. See the related discussion on "wholism or holism" on 109.

Theologians interpret the experience of the life-world according to the epistemological norms of their period. Thomas Aquinas, whose interpretation was greatly influenced by Aristotle, teaches that human knowledge comes through one's native capacity to know and through one's experience (Lane 1989, 15). Finbar Connolly (1991) contrasts certain religious concepts that illustrate the difference between classical knowledge and phenomenological being.

Contrasted understanding

TRADITIONAL UNDERSTANDING	CONCEPT	CONTEMPORARY UNDERSTANDING
Once long ago	Creator	Even now
A fact	Incarnation	A principle
A price paid	Redemption	A way travelled
Gift of grace	New creation	Indwelling person

Guaranteed teacher	Church	Spirit-filled people
Heaven achieved	Salvation	Communion with God and all men
Source of grace	Sacraments	Moment of worship
Legal norms	Morality	Personal values

A relational epistemology (an eidetic epistemology) is a phenomenological understanding of social and cultural symbols which have not lost their power to convince (Tillich 1965, 88). Since phenomenological interpretation is symbolically (socially) constructed, Kaufman (1990, 38) writes that "we must seek to see human existence in terms of these symbolical constructions." Our symbols need to be susceptible to interpretation, otherwise they have no meaning, that is, they need a context or they cannot be reflective of the human experience (Searle 1984, 31). Concerning Christian symbols, Tillich (1965, 97) writes: "no symbol should be removed. It should be reinterpreted." Signs, unlike symbols, are not open to interpretation. Signs admit no contextual nuance. By virtue of its presence a 'stop' sign or a 'no entry' sign signifies that agreed-upon significance regardless of location or context. Symbols, not signs, present themselves as a threshold for phenomenological interpretation. In short, the classical sign shifts to the phenomenological symbol.

6. Third threshold: Idealistic language and interpretation shifts to participatory language and understanding

I follow Zuurdeeg's (1960, 2) interpretation that "*theological* language is convictional language of a special type" [Zuurdeeg's italics]. But it is not necessarily confessional language according to Botha (1990, 14). I further suggest that theological convictional language is unique due to its participatory, not descriptive, character. Paul Tillich (1965, 2) held the same opinion. Further, theological language defies conventional semantics, according to Raschke (1979, 57), and is "self-consciously revelatory." In identifying the field of participational theology, Küng (1988, 116) writes that "*What is at stake here is our everyday, common, human, ambiguous experiences*: not, as in earlier theology, the elitist experiences of intellectual clerics" [Küng's italics]. Baum (1967, 7) says that "many Christians of our day desire to speak about the reality in which they believe in a language and in terms that are in continuity with ordinary experiences of life."

Yet, according to Hay (quoted by Coxhead 1985, 26), most people do not use a religious or theological language that reflects contemporary life experience. Hay writes: "If they do not use traditional religious language, most people are struck dumb when they try to describe the meaning of their experience." Peters (1971, 30) suggests that a problem with personal theological participation lies in its scientific/empirical presentation.

The mistake is to assert that theology can only understand God as a personal being who plans, creates and loves, while at the same time claiming that one should evaluate statements about God coming out of such an understanding by using a method that is not compatible with this view of God, namely the empirical method based on sense experience.

Van den Heever (1993, 43) suggests: " 'God' is the name given to the attempt to guarantee truth by anchoring it outside the flow of discourse in a transcendental signifier." However, MacGregor (1959, 243) opposes a non-personal interpretation. He argues that Kierkegaard's understanding of God as "pure subjectivity" is a personal understanding since only persons can be subjective. Further, he suggests that the "psychological resistance" offered to God is unlikely to be offered to a mere idea about God. I follow McMurrin's (1982, 161) understanding on the personhood of God:

That the philosopher's God, who is the explanation of the world, need not be a person; and the sanction of moral virtue need not be a personal God; but that the God of religion is a person; that, if there is a personal God, religion as it has been known to us in Western culture is true.

In other words the God encountered existentially (in practice) is personal.

Winquist (1975, 105) suggests that phenomenologically understanding existence through the word of God shifts our threshold of interpretation. Dewart (1989, 315), in a footnote, writes that the Berkeleyan view *esse est percipi* (being is perception) would be better rendered had Berkeley written *esse est referri* (being is relational). *Esse est referri* is preferred since phenomenological interpretation involves a relationship. According to Macquarrie (1975, 91), our lifestyle discloses our understanding of that which is divine through a participatory relationship.

Phenomenological theological understanding is an artistic (poetic) work which, in Kaufman's (1990, 33) words, "is to be *lived in*: it is the very form and meaning of human life which is here being constructed and reconstructed" [Kaufman's italics]. Theological artistic (poetic) understanding, as a new threshold, is a participatory form of interpretation. Murray (1975, 80) articulates a phenomenological participation in artistry this way:

> Receiving the truth as an event that casts me in a new situation is the work of interpretation. In interpretation we attempt to articulate this experience with its source in the work of art; to place the self in a position to be claimed by the work, to hear what it says, to enter the realm of its sway.

Theological phenomenological participation is "akin to that of the artist" and is not to be understood merely scientifically (Peters 1971, 47). Theological artistry is not to be understood as re-producing or re-presenting something. Rather, it is to be understood as expressive of an original encounter in a new threshold. Puthanangady (1990, 329) writes that, in liturgical theological interpretation, "original experience is given a new expression in such a way that the people will not only know the content of the original experience, but will be able to have their own experience of it." That is to say, participate in it. Tillich (1965, 39) suggests that the phenomenological interpretation of, or participation in, the life-world occurs "probably more by poetry, drama, and literature than through the visual arts." Concerning the appropriateness of the use of art forms in phenomenological investigation, Mouton and Marais (1990, 176) state that "art forms are frequently employed in investigations such as these as part of the data that is used."

Since poetic constructions are presented in structures peculiar to a given culture, poetry is capable of communal acceptance within that culture. However, no artistic conception originating in a given culture seems capable of translation to other cultures without serious adaptation by, or alteration to, the receiving culture. In short, no universal poetic constructions exist, only particular poetic constructions. There needs to be a shift to a new threshold for each culture. For many individuals in western culture, poetry and philosophy are held to be mutually exclusive. Gilbert Murray (1922, 111), in an essay entitled, 'Poesis and Mimesis,' notes that Aristotle held poetry to be for our "delight" and not to be held as a "criticism of life."

The language of story-telling can become popular and generalized to the point that it is no longer helpful but becomes "pop-theology," a useless threshold. Bloom (1987, 342) understands that "pop-theology" arises when culture presents an ambiguous religious context. Gilson (1968, 248) remarks that "we already have a *pop-psy*; we shall perhaps have to do with a *pop-the*." Bloom (1987, 342) provides this example resulting from cultural ambiguity.

Nobody is quite certain of what the religious institutions are supposed to do anymore, but they do have some kind of role either responding to a real human need or as the vestige of what was once a need, and they invite the exploitation of quacks, adventurers, cranks and fanatics. But they also solicit the warmest and most valiant efforts of persons of peculiar gravity and depth.

Phenomenological understanding is not to be confused with, or equated to, "pop-theology." A challenge for phenomenological artistic theology is to bring to consciousness a personal understanding that is not "pop-theology." Nor is "pop-theology" to be classed with what Jordaan and Jordaan discuss as folk religion. The former is in fact unhelpful to society, whereas the latter "functions in accordance with strict and traditional tribal custom" (Jordaan & Jordaan 1989, 832). Thinking along lines similar to Jordaan and Jordaan, Segundo (1973, 130 & 144) writes:

> it is "popular religion" that fulfils the social functions....And these functions take on a visceral force when truly profound and rapid cultural changes (e.g. urbanization) leave people without the security of an ancestral tradition...."popular religion" is not "popular religiosity" which deforms Christianity.

Torrance (1971, 46) chastises the pop-theologians for contributing to theological confusion. He writes: "This is one of the most insidious problems we have to face in modern theology, where 'pop-theologians' compete with one another in the clamour for demotic adulation and notoriety."

Also, Ebeling (1979, 123) observes: "Today practical theology is faced particularly with the danger of becoming a playground for theological fashion designers and their experiments." As a caution against pop-thelogy, Lonergan (1974, 236) writes the following in an article entitled 'Revolution in Catholic Theology:'

> Neither the scientist nor the philosopher has at his disposal a set of necessary and self-evident truths. He has to observe external nature. He has to attend to his own internal operations and their relations to one another. Neither the observing nor the attending reveals necessity. They merely provide the data in which insight may discern possible relationships, and which further experience may confirm as *de facto* valid.

Despite reservations about a phenomenological philosophy ,the Second Vatican Council did tolerate a phenomenological understanding. In giving a qualified approval, the Council's pastoral constitution, *Gaudium et Spes,* (Art 62) admits that "recent studies and findings of science, history, and philosophy raise new questions which influence life and demand new theological investigations." Further, Abbott (1966, 268), in a footnote to Article 26 remarks that the Council had the intention of "more than a rephrasing of conventional theological teaching in contemporary terminology." I interpret "more than a rephrasing" to mean that a phenomenological understanding (participation in life) is implicitly approved by the Council for Catholic theologians. Ryba (1991, xiv) holds the same view. Dulles (1992, 121) maintains that, in the end, Vatican II did subscribe to phenomenology as its dominant method of understanding. Ryba (1991, iv) makes a stronger statement: "the council itself was *self-consciously* an exercise in the application of the phenomenological method to church doctrine" [Ryba's italics]. Based on this self-conscious initiative John Kobler (2000) presents phenomenological arguments to the traditional Roman perspective. However, in a reactionary move, John Paul II (1993, 9) writes in *Veritatis Splendor* (Art 4) that

> in particular, note should be taken on the *lack of harmony between the traditional response of the Church and certain theological positions*...these being left to the judgment of the individual subjective conscience or to the diversity of social and cultural contexts [John Paul's italics].

It seems that John Paul's encyclical opposes a phenomenological method of understanding. However, it is individualism to which he is opposed in whatever philosophical or social context.

Since classical theology in its contemporary form, labelled Neo-Thomism, often fails to satisfy, a new renaissance can be discerned in western theological thinking in which existential theology is beginning to replace classical theology. A unique insight, peculiar to the phenomenological method, is the conception of knowledge arising from a personal conscious act. In phenomenology, to know is to be conscious.

WORKS CONSULTED

Abbott, W. M. 1966. *Documents of Vatican II.* New York: Guild.

Avis, P. 1990. *Christians in communion.* London: Geoffrey Chapman Mowbray.

Baum, G. 1967. Orthodoxy Recast. In *The future of belief debate,* edited by G. Baum, 103 -8, New York: Herder.

Bent, C. N. 1969. *Interpreting the doctrine of God.* New Jersey: Paulist.

Berger, P. L. 1980. *The heretical imperative: Contemporary possibilities of religious affirmation.* New York: Anchor/Doubleday.

Bloom, A. 1987. *The closing of the American mind: How higher education has failed democracy and impoverished the souls of today's students.* New York: Simon & Schuster.

Botha, C. 1990. *The cave of Adullam or Achor, a door of hope? A history of the faculty of theology of the university of South Africa.* Pretoria: University of South Africa.

Brunner, E. 1942. *Man in revolt: A Christian anthropology.* London: Lutterworth.

Capps, D. 1984. *Pastoral care and hermeneutics.* Philadelphia: Fortress.

Connolly, F. 1991. Change in Theology. Lecture notes distributed at the Priestly Ministry Course. Marianella Pastoral Centre: Dublin, Ireland.

Coxhead, M. 1985. *The relevance of bliss. A contemporary exploration of mystic experience.* London: Wildwood House.

Dewart, L. 1989. *Evolution and consciousness: The role of speech in the origin and development of human nature.* Toronto: University of Toronto Press.

Dillenberger, J. 1969. *Contours of faith: Changing forms of Christian thought.* New York: Abingdon.

Dondeyne, A. 1963. *Contemporary European thought and Christian faith.* Pittsburgh: Duquesne University Press.

Dulles, A. 1992. *The craft of theology: From symbol to system.* New York: Crossroad.

Ebeling, G. 1979. *The study of theology.* London: Collins.

Endean, P. 2000. The Responsibility of Theology for Spiritual Growth and Pastoral Care. *New Blackfriars* 81 (947): 47- 56.

Ferguson, K. 1992. *Stephen Hawking: Quest for a theory of everything.* New York: Bantam.

Garbett, C. 1947. *The claims of the Church of England.* London: Hodder & Stoughton.

Gilkey, L. 1969. *Naming the whirlwind: The renewal of God-language.* New York:Bobbs-Merrill.

—, 1975. *Catholicism confronts modernity: A Protestant view.* New York: Crossroad.

Gilson, E. 1968. On Behalf of the Handmaid. In *Renewal of Religious Thought,* edited by L. K. Shook, 236-49. (Theology of Renewal Vol. 1). Montréal: Palm. Graham, R. 1990. *God's dominion: A sceptic's quest.* Toronto: McClelland & Stewart.

Habermas, J. 1992. *The philosophical discourse of modernity: Twelve lectures.* Cambridge: MIT Press.

Heelan, P. A. 1977. Hermeneutics of Experimental Science in the Context of the Life-world. In *Interdisciplinary phenomenology,* edited by D. Ihde and R. Zaner, 7-50. The Hague: Martinus Nijhoff.

Hofmeyr, J. 1979. Religion in the Interpretation of Experience. PhD thesis. University of Cape Town. (Unpublished)

Hinners, R. C. 1967. The Challenge of Dehellenization. In *The future of belief debate*, edited by G. Baum, 197-208. New York: Herder & Herder.

Hurley, M. 1969. *Theology of ecumenism*. Notre Dame: Fides. (Theology Today Series 9.)

John Paul II. 1993. *Veritatis Splendor*. (Encyclical letter addressed to all the bishops of the Catholic Church regarding certain fundamental questions of the church's moral teaching). Ottawa: Canadian Conference of Catholic Bishops.

—, 1994. *Crossing the threshold of hope*, ed by Vittorio Messori. New York: Alfred Knopf.

Jordaan, W. and J. Jordaan. 1989. *Man in context*. Johannesburg: Lexicon.

Kaufman, G. 1990. *An essay on theological method*. Atlanta, Georgia: Scholars Press.

Keen, E. 1970. *Three faces of being: Toward an existential clinical psychology*. New York: Appleton-Century-Crofts.

King, W. L. 1968. *Introduction to religion: A phenomenological approach*. New York: Harper & Row.

Kobler, J. 2000. Vatican II theology needs philosophy. *The Modern Schoolman* LXXIII (1): 89-95.

Koestenbaum, P. 1967. Religion in the Tradition of Phenomenology. In *Religion in philosophical and cultural perspective: A new approach to the philosophy of religion through cross-disciplinary studies.* edited by C. J. Feaver and W. Horosz, 174-214. Princeton, New Jersey: D Van Nostrand.

Küng, H. 1988. *Theology for the third millenium: An ecumenical view*. New York: Doubleday.

Kurtz, L. R.1986. *The politics of heresy: The modernist crisis in Roman Catholicism*. Los Angeles: University of California Press.

Lane, D. 1989. *The experience of God: An invitation to do theology*. Dublin: Veritas.

Laycock, S. W. 1986. Introduction: To ward an Overview of Phenomenological Theology. In *Essays in phenomenological theology,* edited by S. W. Laycock and J. G. Hart, 1-22. New York: State University Press.

Liderbach, D. 2001. Modernism in the Roman church. *Explorations: Journal for Adventurous Thought* 20 (1): 17-36.

Lonergan, B. 1969. The Absence of God in Modern Culture. In *The Presence and Absence of God,* edited by C. Mooney, 164-178). New York: Fordham University Press.

-, 1974. A Second Collection. *A second collection,* edited by W. F. Ryan and B. J. Tyrrell, 101-16. London: Darton, Longman & Todd.

—, 1972. *Method in theology.* New York: Herder & Herder.

Lowe, D. M. 1982. *History of bourgeous perception.* Chicago: University of Chicago Press.

MacGregor, G. 1959. *Introduction to religious philosophy.* Boston: Houghton Mifflin.

Macquarrie, J. 1975. *Thinking about God.* New York: Harper & Row.

Mallard, W. 1977. *The reflection of theology in literature: A case study in theology and culture.* San Antonio, Texas: Trinity University Press.

Maurer, A. 1967. Dewart's de-hellenization of belief in God. *The Ecumenist* 5: 22-5.

Maxwell, P. 1986. Some reflections on the so-called phenomenological method in the study of religion. *Religion in Southern Africa* 7: 15-25.

McMurrin, S. M. 1982. *Religion, reason, and truth: Historical essays in the philosophy of religion.* Salt Lake City: University of Utah Press.

Merleau-Ponty, M. 1964. *Sense and Non-sense.* Evanston: Northwestern University Press.

Möeller, C 1968. Renewal of the Doctrine of Man In *Renewal of religious structures,* edited by L. K. Shook, 420-63. Montréal: Palm.

Morreall, J. 1983. Can theological language have hidden meaning? *Religious Studies* 19: 43-56.

Mouton, J. and H. C. Marais. 1990. *Basic concepts in the methodology of the social sciences.* South Africa: Human Sciences Research Council. (HSRC Series in Methodology 4.)

Murray G. 1922. *Essays and Addresses.* London: George Allen & Unwin.

—, 1940. *Stoic, Christian and humanist.* London: C. A. Watts.

Murray, M. 1975. *Modern critical theory: A phenomenological introduction.* The Hague: Martinus Nijhoff.

Neville, R. C. 1991. *Behind the masks of God: An essay toward comparative theology.* Albany, New York: State University of New York Press.

Nipkow, K. E. 1993. Empirical research within practical theology. *Journal of Empirical Theology* 6: 50-63.

Ott, H. 1967. Language and understanding. In *New theology 4,* edited by M. E. Marty and D. G. Peerman, 124-146. New York: Macmillan.

Peters, K. E. 1971. The concept of God and the method of science: An exploration of the possibility of scientific theology. PhD thesis, Columbia University, New York.

Pieterse, H. 1994. The empirical approach in practical theology: A discussion with J A van der Ven. *Religion and Theology* 1: 77-83.

Platt, D. 1989. *Intimations of divinity.* New York: Peter Lang.

Prentice, R. 1971. The expanding universe of spirit in Dewart's 'religion, language and truth.' *The Ecumenist* 10: 25-30.

Puthanangady, P. 1990. Cultural Elements in Liturgical Prayers. In *Shaping English liturgy: Studies in honour of Archbishop Denis Hurley*, edited by P. C. Finn and J. M. Schellman, 327-39. Washington: Pastoral Press.

Raschke, C. 1979. *The alchemy of the word: Language and the end of theology*. Atlanta, American Academy of Religion: Studies in Religion 20.)

Robinson, J. A. 1967. *Exploration into God*. Stanford: Stanford University Press.

Robinson, J. M. and J. B. Cobb. 1963. *The later Heidegger and theology*. New York: Harper Row.

Ryba, T. 1991. *The essence of phenomenology and its meaning for the scientific study of religion*. New York: Peter Lang.

Searle, J. 1984. *Minds, brains and science*. London: Penguin.

Seasoltz, K. R. 1983. The Sacred liturgy: Development and Directions. In *Remembering the future: Vatican II and tomorrow's liturgical agenda*, edited by C. A. Last, 48-79. New York: Paulist.

Segundo, J. L. 1973. *Our idea of God*. New York: Orbis.

Seidel, J. 1991. Method and Madness in the Application of Computer Technology to Qualitative Data Analysis. In *Using computers in qualitative research,* edited by N. G. Fielding and R. M. Lee, 107-16. London: Sage.

Shea, J. 1980. Introduction: Experience and symbol, an approach to theologizing. *Chicago Studies* 19, 5-20.

Sontag, F. 1969. *The future of theology: A philosophical basis for contemporary Protestant thought*. Philadelphia: Westminster.

Stanton, G. N. 1989. *The gospels and Jesus*. Oxford: Oxford University Press.

Steyn, C. 1994. Responsibility as an element in new age consciousness. *Religion and Theology* 1: 283-91.

Streng, F. 1991. Purposes and investigative principles in the phenomenology of religion: A reconstruction. *Journal for the Study of Religion* 4: 3-17.

Tillich, P. 1965. *Ultimate concern: Tillich in dialogue*. New York: Harper.

Torrance, T. 1969. *Theological science*. London: Oxford University Press.

—, 1971. *God and rationality*. London: Oxford University Press.

Tymieniecka, A. T. 1962. *Phenomenology and science in contemporary European thought*. New York: Noonday.

Tyrrell, G. 1907. *Through Scylla and Charybdis or the old theology and the new*. London: Longmans, Green.

Van den Heever, G. 1993. Being and nothingness. *Theologica Evangelica* 1:39-47.

Vanhoozer, K. J. 1993. Is the World well staged? Theology, Culture, and Hermeneutics. In *God and culture: Essays in honor of Carl F H Henry*, edited by D. A. Carson and J. D. Woodbridge, 1-30. Grand Rapids, Michigan: Eerdmans.

Waardenburg, J. D. 1973. Research on Meaning in Religion. In *Religion, culture and methodology*, edited by Th. P. Van Baaren and H. J. W. Drijvers, 109-36. The Hague: Mouton.

Wild, J. 1964. Husserl's Life-world and the Lived Body. In *Phenomenology: Pure and applied*, edited by E. W. Straus, 10-42. Pittsburgh: Duquesne University Press.

Winquist, C. E. 1975. *The communion of possibility*. Chico, California: New Horizons.

Zuurdeeg, W. F. 1960. The nature of theological language. *Journal of Religion* 40: 1-8.

GLOSSARY OF TERMS

compensation: an individual's attempt to overcome feelings of inferiority through adaptation.

conscious: part of the mind of which an individual is currently aware.

creative power of the self: the ability that individuals have to create their own lifestyle.

ego: mediates between the *id* and *superego* trying to satisfy the desires of the *id* while obeying the restraints of external conditions (i.e., operating on the reality principle) and the superego.

ego psychology: school of personality development based on the premise that the ego existed separate from the *id*.

id: the most primitive and primal motivating force of the human psyche, which operates on the pleasure principle.

inferiority complex: an inability to solve life's problems. Being unable to compensate for one's inadequacies in a positive co-operative manner which would promote social tolerance.

false consensus effect: tendency to overestimate the commonality of an individual's own opinions, behaviors, or experiences.

fictional finalism: decisions are based on predictions of what is likely to happen in the future. Individuals act on the "as if" principle. They act "as if" certain ideals are real. The future is fictive although individuals see it as an entity or possibility.

organ inferiority: feelings of inferiority arising from a physiological deficit of some kind.

overcompensation: exaggerated striving or striving in inappropriate ways.

preconscious: part of the mind just out of awareness, which can be accessed with effort.

private logic: neurotic, yet subjectively logical, reasoning and behaviour used to deal with the perceived demands of the world.

social interest (social feeling): the need to live in harmony with others in society. "The individual only lives successfully by willing cooperation with others and being deeply concerned with the welfare of others. . . . [Individuals] are essentially fully responsible for [their] own behaviours."

social tolerance: a measure of social interest. An individual's ability to co-operate with others and work toward bettering humanity.

striving for superiority: the act of compensating for feelings of inferiority by moving towards a specific ideal or fictional finalism.

style of life (lifestyle): consists of both concerns over inferiority feelings and the patterns of behaviour an individual develops to deal with these feelings in his or her striving for superiority. Each lifestyle is logical and rational, although it can be mistaken. Mistaken lifestyles lead to neurosis in an individual.

superego: enforces societal values impressed upon an individual by the parents — basically, an individual's conscience.

unconscious: part of the mind not directly accessible and of which an individual is largely unaware.

BIOGRAPHICAL INFORMATION

Allan Savage earned his Doctorate in the subject of Practical Theology at the University of South Africa. Ordained Roman Catholic priest in 1978 he currently serves as Chaplain to Thunder Bay Regional Hospital, Thunder Bay, Ontario and represents the Ontario Conference of Catholic Bishops to the Ontario Mulitifaith Council on Spiritual and Religious Care. A sessional lecturer in the Faculty of Theology, University of Winnipeg, he has written articles in *Explorations: Journal for Adventurous Thought, The Canadian Journal of Adlerian Psychology, Year Book 2001* (Adlerian Society of the United Kingdom and the institute for Individual Psychology), and in the online journals: *Quodlibet: Online Journal of Christian Theology and Philosophy* [www.Quodlibet.net] and *OMNI: Journal of Spiritual and Religious Care* [www.omc.on.ca]. His first book is entitled: *A Phenomenological Understanding of Certain Liturgical Texts: The Anglican Collects for Advent and the Roman Catholic Collects for Lent.*

Born in Stephenville, Newfoundland, Sheldon Nicholl was raised in Pasadena, Newfoundland — a town on the province's west coast near the city of Corner Brook. He holds an honors degree in Psychology and a degree in Canadian English Literature from Sir Wilfred Grenfell College (Memorial University of Newfoundland's west coast campus). He received his masters degree in clinical psychology from Lakehead University in Thunder Bay, Ontario. He presently resides in St. John's, Newfoundland where he works as a clinical psychologist with the Psychiatric Rehabilitation Team. This inter-disciplinary team consisting of several disciplines (psychology, psychiatry, social work, occupational therapy, recreational therapy, nursing, pastoral care) provides psychological assessments and treatment for clients as well as provides case management services. His clinical interests lie in addictions, (the understanding of drug self-administration, the determination of factors contributing to the changes in use of alcohol and other drugs during the lifespan, and factors affecting the extent of drug use in youth), pain studies and health care delivery issues related to persons suffering from uncontrolled pain, psycho-oncology, and traumatology. This work represents his first publication and attempt at co-authorship.

Erik Mansager was born in Montevideo, Minnesota but was raised in the deserts of southern Arizona. His bachelor's degree was earned at St. Thomas Theological Seminary in Denver, Colorado. He earned his master's degree in marriage and family counseling from the University of Arizona, mentored by Oscar Christensen, Rudolf Dreikurs's protégée. Erik wrote his master's thesis on the interrelationship between self-actualization and lifestyles among Catholic priests. His doctorate in the psychology of religion was earned at the Catholic University of Leuven, Belgium. He is the guest editor of a special issue of the Journal of Individual Psychology on "Holism, Wellness, and Spirituality" (56:3, 2000). At different times he served at St. John's Seminary College, Los Angeles, as its Director of Psychological Services and as its Academic dean. Currently he is the Director of the Student Counseling Center at the University of North Dakota.

Anita Oja was born in Boras, Sweden and has lived in Canada since childhood. After graduating from York University with a degree in Science she moved to Thunder Bay, Ontario and obtained a degree in Education at Lakehead University. From 1983 to 1997, she taught Physics and Mathematics on a sessional basis in the Technology Division at Confederation College in Thunder Bay. Recently she led off-campus seminar courses for the Faculty of Theology at the University of Winnipeg. The seminar courses were: *God and Science,* and *Christianity and Art.* These eclectic courses mirror her interests in the synergy of science, theology, philosophy and the arts – she is a part-time student in the Honours Bachelor of Visual Arts programme. "To stop learning is to stop living."

Index

INDEX OF NAMES